Too Much Religion is Bad For Your Faith

by

Richard King

authorHOUSE®

AuthorHouse™
1663 Liberty Drive, Suite 200
Bloomington, IN 47403
www.authorhouse.com
Phone: 1-800-839-8640

This book is a work of non-fiction. Unless otherwise noted, the author and the publisher make no explicit guarantees as to the accuracy of the information contained in this book and in some cases, names of people and places have been altered to protect their privacy.

First published by AuthorHouse   10/7/2008

ISBN: 978-1-4389-1628-6 (sc)

Printed in the United States of America
Bloomington, Indiana

This book is printed on acid-free paper.

TABLE OF CONTENTS

Chapter 1
RELIGION AND FAITH

The Obsession

ONCE upon a time there was an Obsession. It was born in a land far away and grew daily until it became larger than life; and still it went on growing. Before long it obscured the sun, and even the rain clouds, from that whole land so there was continual darkness and it never rained. There was great consternation as the crops failed and the people began to starve; in desperation they consulted the king himself, yet even the king in all his majesty was powerless in the face of so great an Obsession. Meanwhile it grew so large it could no longer move but wallowed where it was and quivered like a jelly. And still it grew.

At the same time there was a little seed, the seed of a hawthorn. It struggled to germinate and struggled harder still to grow, there was so little light and even less water. Yet bit by agonising bit it grew to become a tiny bush, a bush which nevertheless had exceedingly sharp thorns. As the bush grew these thorns began to dig into the softest part of the Obsession until one day, with an enormous bang, it burst. The sound of the explosion reached the inside of the royal palace where the king leapt out of bed in a fright to discover that it was not the middle of the night, as he had thought, but high noon. The Obsession was so insubstantial there was almost nothing left of it except a shred here and there.

How the people of that land cheered. The king declared a holiday and in gratitude his subjects carried him on their shoulders all round his kingdom. There were fireworks and there was feasting and everyone said what a great king they had; for now the sun could shine and the rain fall and the crops could grow. In their excitement no one noticed the little hawthorn. But over time the bush became a beautiful tree with little white flowers which shaded only enough of the sun to provide cool for passing travellers, and shielded only enough rain to offer shelter to poor stragglers.

In time the king died and the prince took his place, children grew old, a new generation arose and there was no one left who could remember the Obsession, except in an increasingly elaborate fable in which the brave king himself fought the Obsession single-handed with only the aid of a lance and five thousand horse guards. Unnoticed the tree flourished, grew old and, after many years, it died. God Himself welcomed the tree into heaven. "Well done, my thorny friend," He whispered, "it was your prickles made the sun shine and the rain fall, and allowed all kinds of flowers to grow."

<hr />

WHEN I wrote this story I had in mind rather mundane obsessions; but, as with any half-decent story, I soon discovered that there are other layers of meaning in it. The writer, as also the composer or painter with their music and pictures, is not always the best person to understand his or her own story. For a start I learnt that, apparently, the hawthorn represents "true love, partnership and commitment".[1] I found too, with the help of a friend, that the Obsession in my story could stand for a rather grander, corporate compulsion, for example, religion.

The wife of a Church of England Bishop was wont to say at episcopal dinner parties, "Too much religion is bad for your faith." It was a suitable corrective to a table full of aspiring young clergy all outdoing one another in ecclesiastical piety.

So I wondered; if in my story the Obsession were to turn out to be religion, what would be the significance of the little hawthorn which ultimately pricks the bubble? Part of the purpose of my book is to attempt an answer to this question.

<hr />

ONE of my dearest friends, indeed the friend who opened my eyes to the deeper significance of my story, is a prisoner on Death Row in Florida. His name is Charles Globe and his number is 097707. Charles has been in prison for 23 years, initially for a crime he can now show he didn't commit. For this "crime" he received two life sentences plus thirty years. In the USA "life" means life. After 16 years in prison Charles killed another prisoner and for this received a death sentence. Over the last few years Charles has been growing in faith and the growth has accelerated of late. We shall meet Charles again in chapter 5.

Monica, my wife, and I have grown to love Charles and he loves us. When we recently moved house I wanted to describe our new home to Charles and so I wrote him a story about an imagined visit from Charles to our home. This is the beginning of my story.

Our Visitor

MELTON Mowbray station once knew more glorious days; in its heyday there was a through train to London. Now the goods yards are overgrown; an elderly manual signal box and semaphore signals give joy to train-spotters if not signalmen and two- or sometimes three-car diesel units provide the passenger service from Birmimgham. As the evening train squealed to a halt and the doors opened I felt a nervous thrill; I scanned the faces of the disembarking passengers; Charles was the last off the train, he stepped with a swing onto the platform wearing a tight T-shirt and carrying a hold-all. He looked tired after the transat-lantic flight but there was a curious light around his face.

"Hi, Buddy." He smiled, we embraced and looked in disbelief into each other's faces and then walked to the waiting car. Five minutes later we arrived at our home. I carried Charles' bag into the hall...

AFTER I wrote this story I almost came to believe Charles may one day visit our house, so much so that I found myself saying to my wife that Charles could do this or that "when he comes." Stories, even stories like this one, have this power. In this case, though, it is nothing but wishful thinking and a device to describe our home to someone who will never see it for himself. But suppose we told a similar story about another guest, this time in a fragment of a poem.

The House (part)

In some street there's a house,
        Somewhere.
Just an ordinary house, small
        Rather dark.
But inside there are rooms beyond
        Curtained rooms
Where no one ever goes.

One night a man arrives and stays a while ...[2]

PART of my purpose in this book, as I have already mentioned, is to answer the question of the identity of the hawthorn in my first story. Another purpose is to begin to imagine those unexplored rooms and what the unexpected visitor talked about during his stay. And there's more.

IN 1952 the experimental composer John Cage wrote a piano piece entitled 4'33". In this piece the performer sits at the piano but doesn't play a note and the whole is to last just over four and a half minutes or some other time. This might seem like a gimmick and certainly it can bear no imitation but there is a serious purpose, viz to understand that all the sounds around us are, ultimately, music; and to get the audience really listening to those sounds. Cage's music is the music of the gaps, in other words what happens in the rests. Another purpose in my book is to listen to what happens in the gaps, in the rests, the subtle sounds hidden away where few if any will look for them. Curiously music is the most abstract of creative media, yet the sounds in those gaps are "real" enough, even if the person who "recently" assisted in a test in the Royal Festival Hall hasn't got a cough.[3] In fact it is the "still small voice", or the "sound of silence."

THIS is a profoundly anti-religious book. But before religious people jump up and down too vigorously I must define how I am using the term "religion". The noun "religion" and its adjective "religious" have several meanings. We use "religion" to distinguish between different belief systems, say Christianity and Hinduism. This is a precise usage and I have no problem with it. Within Christianity "religious" is properly used to distinguish the particular form of discipleship we sometimes call monasticism. Again this is precise and I have no problem with it. However, in popular use the words "religion" and "religious" are associated with a form of piety which has, by and large, lost all credibility. "Religion" or "religious" subtly suggest rigid doctrines, even mindless fanaticism and, as it were, faith by numbers. Religions, by this definition, are made up of rules and doctrines; keep the rules, believe the doctrines, however unlikely, and you keep in with your particular deity. Recite the Creed, learn the Catechism, go to church, it's all so much easier than the real thing. Now, as I shall suggest in chapter 8, discipline is an important part of faith, but it is not a substitute for it; in fact, when religion gets substituted for faith wars start, bonfires are lit (for the purpose of burning books if not people) and middle-aged women fall out over the jam stall at the church fête. When religion takes the place of faith honest believers are excommunicated over homosexuality and women's ordination, or else their failure to believe in the virginal conception. When I use the term "religion" this is the meaning I have in mind.

5

RELIGION is news. For many people the term is closely associated with fundamentalism or even terrorism. In his recent book *The God Delusion* [4] Richard Dawkins, despite the title, attacks religion more than he attacks God. As far as that goes, I agree with him. Dreadful things have been done in the name of religion, torture, persecution, war and terrorism among others. Most of us can see the absurdity of the more deluded forms of religion; and it's fun to ridicule, as Dawkins does, the mad excesses of some "religious" leaders. There is a rich vein to mine as anyone who has ever watched American TV will know. I conclude, perhaps even more thoroughly than Dawkins, that "religion" itself is at fault. So where does that leave those of us who believe in God? And what is the antidote to religion?

In 1988, when I first began to lead the five session prayer workshop I now call *Closer to God* one of only five participants in the very first course was Doreen, a widow of seventy. When the five weeks were over she said, "I've been coming to church all my life and I never knew God could speak to me." Dangerous delusion or exciting liberation? We could let Doreen's actions speak for themselves. Despite her age and respectability Doreen began, not only to pray in a new way, she also began to visit strangers and tell them of her faith. Quite soon she abandoned the formal religion of the Parish church and became a founder member of a new community of faith, a "church plant", which met in a pub on a rough council estate; this new church was partly the result of her visiting. When, a year or two later, she died quite suddenly, her funeral was one of the most joyful I can remember, at which we rejected "Abide with me" in favour of "Shine, Jesus, Shine" and the organ in favour of drums.

At about the same time I was visited in the Vicarage by a group of similarly elderly ladies who were concerned that our church was abandoning the religious conventions with which they had grown up. They were disturbed that so much they had assumed to be essential was being abandoned. I listened carefully to their complaint, but I had a suggestion for them. I suggested that the three of them get together every week to pray for the church. It is a testimony to their openness that they agreed, and they set to work the same week. Within a short time they were transformed and so was the church. I thought then, as I think now, that they were the engine which drove it along. Prayer does that. The image of the swan is well-known but most apt in this context: They were the hard working but unseen legs which enabled the church to glide apparently effortlessly along. I recently wrote to the Presiding Bishop of the Episcopal Church of the USA and the Archbishop of the Church of Nigeria suggesting that their religious differences would best be resolved if they were to go on retreat and pray together. I received a courteous personally signed reply from one and nothing from the other, you will have to guess which was which.

Over the years over a thousand people have taken part in these *Closer to God* workshops, often in groups of forty or fifty, most often from traditional churches and, while it doesn't "work" for everyone, a significant number of people have experienced liberation through it; they have been set free from the dead hand, the obsession, of religion; they have discovered something different, something alive, something which can transform. We might, perhaps, tentatively associate what they discovered with the little hawthorn. The parallel is appropriate because what they discovered is no anodyne piety, no comfort blanket, nor an easy option. They discovered something infinitely beautiful but which can, at the same time, prick the bubble of hypocrisy, lance the boil of pomposity, destroy for ever the smug mediocrity which passes for religion in many a church. What was it? I will call it "Faith".

———•◆•———

FOR me, faith involves following Jesus of Nazareth. His was the first and still the most profound assault on religion. It led Him into serious conflict with the religious people of His day, in particular the Pharisees, and before long it led to an appalling death. Religious people hate women and men of faith, and what they stand for, that much. In the years that followed the death of Jesus His followers certainly upset the secular authorities too and suffered accordingly, but through history the most monstrous excesses have been carried out by religious people, either against each other, or against people of faith. The cause of these enormities is the lack of confidence and integrity which religion encourages.

In his marvellous book, *God of Surprises*,[5] Gerard Hughes describes a picture of God held by many traditional Catholics, though similar pictures could be suggested by members of every other denomination too. Hughes suggests many Catholics see God as like "good old Uncle George"[6]. The man is a monster who imposes his will by sheer terror, the threat of hell. In reality it is not the God and Father of Jesus Christ, who issues these threats, but the church. Why? Because deviation threatens the power of an authoritarian church. It's not only Catholics who struggle with such images, there is also many an Evangelical who feels compelled to cling doggedly to the absolute inerrancy of Scripture in every word, against all logic. They will say something like this, "If one word of Scripture is not 'true' then the whole lot comes tumbling down like a pack of cards." Similarly we could find traditionalists who say that it is necessary for salvation to believe every clause of the Creeds; some hard-liners may even excommunicate a sister or brother who denies the virginal conception; but the heavyweights of the New Testament, Paul and John, don't see fit to mention it. We shall see in chapter 3 just how dangerous creeds can be. For the insecure it is essential that everyone believes the same, often in every detail. Adrian Plass captured this brilliantly in his hilarious (and fictional) *Sacred Diary*.[7] A monk comes to preach at Adrian's church. He says that God is nice and likes people. Adrian comments, "We all looked at Edwin [the leader of the church] to see if we agreed."[8] Insecurity leads to broken integrity as we cling to barely understood and at best partially believed "truths", and thus to fear.

Insecurity is a debilitating state which leads not just to shattered integrity but also to inhuman acts against those seen as a threat. The question is, in whom or what can we find security? Does our security lie in the authority of the Church? Does it reside in the Creeds? Or perhaps it lies in the person of the Pastor or the form of the liturgy, or the style of the hymns or even (one can scarcely believe it) in the position of the pews, or who runs the tombola at the church garden party. I met a priest once who would not receive communion from a colleague because he was not wearing vestments and, he said, "you could not be sure he was 'sound'". In this day, when priests will not receive from their own bishop because of the ordination of women, this has a very sharp edge indeed. Incidentally I see from a recent catalogue that you can still buy clerical cufflinks, sports shorts and golfing trousers; why ever not clerical pyjamas for those emergency night time calls?

Security will not be found in any of these. They are human constructs, hopefully inspired. There is only one place we can find genuine lasting security, in the God of Love Himself, through His Son Jesus. But think, "If God is for us, who can be against us?"[9] If I know that God loves me how can disagreements even about the Bible or the Creeds, or the liturgy or the pews, never mind the jam, disturb my peace? This is faith.

I love the Scriptures, I read the Bible daily and pray with it most days. It is an incomparable gift for people of faith, it speaks to us of Jesus, who is "the radiance of God's glory and the exact representation of his being."[10] I can't say with conviction that I love the Creeds with the same intensity, though I recognise in them an important indicator of faith. I also love the liturgy and many hymns and songs both traditional and contemporary but I recognise their human origins and their mostly transient nature. But none of these pillars of religion, not even the Bible itself which is in an entirely different category to the others, is a firm basis for faith. I hope, before we conclude our journey, we shall discover the firmest of foundations for a life of faith. And this is a journey, not something static. We shall see in chapter 4 that faith, like anything alive, is in constant movement, and so are we. The chapters of this book are a tiny fragment of an eternal journey. Happy travelling.

Endnotes

[1] *The Week* 11th August 2007 p.39

[2] The rest of this poem can be found in chapter 11.

[3] This "recent" test revealed that a cough registers the same number of decibels as a note played *mezzo-forte* on the horn

[4] *The God Delusion* Richard Dawkins (Bantam 2006)

[5] *God of Surprises* Gerard W Hughes (DLT 1985)

[6] *Ibid* p 34

[7] *The Sacred Diary of Adrian Plass (aged 37 ¾)* Adrain Plass (Marshall Pickering 1987)

[8] *Ibid p 8*

[9] Romans 8:31

[10] Hebrews 1:3

Chapter 2

FAITH AS STORY

Grace

He promised to set my spirit free
      From dull and boring mediocrity
      Conformity, respectability,
      Changeless monotony; He
Said my intellect could roam
      Unfettered, free and far from home
      But my thinking mind had almost gone
      To seed,
      Thinking is not considered sound,
      You know.
He told my imagination to soar
      To heavenly places and return for more
      Stimulation. But a TV tube has done
      For that
      And now I'm nothing but a bore.
He sent an invitation to my body to dance
      And like a fool to chance and prance
      Naked, unencumbered,
      On the grass by moonlight.
      But sterner rules are made for fools
      And gossip makes a powerful
      Restraining tool.

The shackles of theology, orthodoxy, morality
      Piety, high tea with the Vicar
Have tightened round the ankles of my soul.
Righteousness, fiery justice and love
      Are "interesting concepts though quite
      Impractical in the modern world
      Of economic management, and prudent
      Policy".

Then suddenly, as if a flash or shiver,
> Quiver of light penetrated the gloom;
> Perhaps a river of insanity flooded
> A heart grown dry with rationality.
An instant clairvoyancy shattered sanity,
> Modesty. A sea
> Of energy rolled over me, making me
> The man I ought to be,
> Returning praise; and He, receiving it,
> Smiled and reached out to bless and yet
> To call to higher sacrifice.

THAT poem is part of my story. But it's not the record of an event and to that extent I suppose it is not really a story at all, rather it is the ongoing struggle in my soul between law and grace, religion and faith. That "flash or shiver" is not a once-for-all milestone, it is part of the continuing pilgrimage of my soul to God. Because it is poetry rather than prose it captures a little of what goes on in my heart rather than in my head. I could tell my story rather differently:

A Story for Christmas Day

LIFE is like a labyrinth. There's a famous circular Labyrinth in Chartres Cathedral, which weaves in and out, back and forth until finally you reach the centre, your destination. On the way you find yourself sometimes passing others going in the opposite direction; other times you walk alongside someone for a while until your paths diverge. Sometimes you walk towards someone only to find, at the last minute, that you both double back; and sometimes you find you are walking with someone you met earlier.

The same applies in life. We meet all kinds of people, some for a moment at a bus stop, others we walk with almost the whole of our lives. But occasionally we meet someone special, someone we never forget, they make a difference to our lives. Most of us can name a handful of people who are really special.

Among my special people is a friend of 34 years. Martin and I have shared most of the highs and lows of each other's lives. Our emerging music careers we shared; I was Martin's Best Man and he was mine, he even conducted my second marriage; we shared the joy of the birth of our children; we shared the awesome call to the ordained ministry. And we shared the pain of my divorce and Martin's close encounter with cancer and death. Friends like Martin change the quality of our lives.

Then there's Josh, unusual name, unusual guy. He's not my oldest friend, I first met him a few years after Martin, but he may be my strangest. I met him on a train - I can still remember the date, 4th November 1974 - I got on and there he was and we fell to talking. He looked – how can I put it? – odd. Shabby clothes and a northern accent; he wore a straggly beard and I could see, even though it was November, that he wore no socks; funny how you remember little things. Yet, for all that, there was a hint of the aristocrat about him too, and he seemed to know about lots of things; he should have been on *Mastermind*. We talked all the way to London and he was just, so interesting. We swapped phone numbers before we left and that's how I got to know Him. When I telephoned he seemed always to be out, but sometimes I would catch him and I even bumped into him occasionally, on Wimbledon Common or somewhere, when I wasn't expecting him. I later discovered that we narrowly missed meeting earlier in my life.

As I got to know him I found he is always the life and soul of a party; he loves a drink and a laugh with friends; but he likes to be quiet with them too. He seems to go to loads of parties and you'll either find him at the bar with a crowd - he has a fund of stories and if he repeats them sometimes they always seem to have a new twist - or else you'd find him tucked away in a corner talking to someone who's just been ditched by her boyfriend. Either way, when Josh is at a party it goes with a swing, people are happier and closer. He loves a practical joke; but not unkindly, never mocking, just sharing the absurdity of life, laughing with the victim not at them. He is the most intense person I know but the most relaxed too. It's not surprising that he has loads of friends and I wonder sometimes whether he remembers who I am, there are so many others. Yet he's one of those people who always knows a name.

And his many friends come from all walks of life. I've seen him underneath the arches at Waterloo, and I saw, in a gossip column, a picture of him at a society ball in Mayfair. He knows politicians and plumbers, and it makes no difference to him, he's the same with them all.

Later I found there is a secret side to Josh, one he doesn't talk about much, his work with the sick and the dying for example. I know a bit about it because I've always found that at the lowest points in my life there have been little messages of encouragement in the post, or a phone call.

I know Josh has lots of friends, all over the world it seems. I can't claim a special relationship, as I can with Monica my wife, or with Martin; yet somehow I do feel special when he's around; he has that effect on people, everyone who knows him says the same. He is simply the most magnetic person in the world.

But I do feel rather privileged today because he's here. I won't blow his cover, but you'll probably know him when you see him. Welcome Josh – and – Happy Birthday, mate.

———·•·———

AFTER I had told that story, at a Christmas Communion service, one of the listeners, a stranger to me, recommended I read a book entitled *Joshua* by Joseph Girzone,[11] which uses rather a similar idea; and even lent me a copy. It's a good book, of which I had been blissfully ignorant until then. But my version is *my* story, not Girzone's, however excellent his book is. The question you may want to ask is this: Is my story true?

That's a difficult question. I would answer strongly, "Yes, it is true." Nevertheless you may argue that there never was a Josh on that train; and if you had been on the same train from Raynes Park to Waterloo, in the same carriage (the front one) I agree you wouldn't have seen anyone sitting with me, nor heard me engage in conversation; but at a much deeper level I met Jesus on that train.

Mine is the story of the day I met Jesus, a variant form of the name Joshua – Josh for short. Girzone's book uses the same disguise to tell the story of Jesus returning to a small community in rural America.

So, have I been lying? I don't think so; I have been using a story to tell a deeper truth. I could have written the whole thing in boring narrative prose. I don't think it would have engaged you, the reader, in the same way, neither would it have got anywhere near portraying the deep down truth of this amazing person, Jesus.

————•◦•————

SO far I have been telling my story. Certainly my story is important, but there are other stories and I don't just mean your stories, which are also important; I mean there are *our* stories, the common stories which bind communities together as they tell and re-tell the story of, for example, their origin, or some episode in their common life. Perhaps the story which has survived in this way for the longest is the story of their escape from Egypt which the Jews tell each other, and re-enact, every Passover; this common story has succeeded in holding together a people through almost inconceivable trials, for several thousand years.

Christians tell each other a story, and re-enact it too, regularly, every day in some cases. It is the story of the death and resurrection of Jesus Christ. We remember and relive this drama every time we celebrate the Eucharist together. "The Lord Jesus, on the night he was betrayed, took bread …."[12] This is our common story, this is the thread which unites and binds all Christians together in one body.[13]

————•◦•————

THE Bible is not one book, it is a library of books. In the library there are all kinds of literature. There is law, there is prophecy, there is poetry and music, philosophy, theology; there are stories and myths, and there is history. We are, of course, concerned in this chapter with stories, but before we can consider them we must be clear that because the Bible contains different sorts of literature we cannot approach it in only one way. That way we get into all kinds of trouble.

The Bible story, the history of God's people actually begins in Genesis 12:1, "The LORD [YHWH] said to Abram ..." A large part of the Old Testament and a chunk of the New tells the history of God's people, the common story about our origins which binds us together with a common identity.

If the story begins in chapter 12, what about the first eleven chapters of Genesis? These are a completely different sort of literature, generally thought to be later in origin than what follows. These stories, the creation (two accounts)[14], the fall, the flood, the tower of Babel among them, are what we call "myths". Now, please don't think this means they are not "true". Myths are a way of conveying truth which uses story in exactly the same way I used story to convey the truth of my own meeting with Jesus. These myths do not attempt a scientific explanation, they attempt to answer such questions as, Where did I come from? Why is there so much sin and suffering in the world? Why are there so many different languages? And in this they use story to allow them to penetrate beneath the level of the head. The religious person will need to tie him- or herself into logical knots to explain the two different accounts of creation. Were human beings created before or after the animals for example?[15] Did God make man and woman together[16] or did He create man first and then woman from man's rib?[17] There is no logical resolution to these dilemmas, until we, as people of faith, see them as poetic, musical stories designed to illustrate a deeper truth.

Certain parts of the Bible are historical narrative. David became King of Israel, for example.[18] However, even history is not as cut and dried as we may like to think. In my day English schoolboys learnt about the battles of Agincourt and Creçy, those who spent time in French schools were puzzled that French children appeared to be utterly ignorant of these "important" battles. I suppose French children who learnt Shakespeare would have to find out at least about Agincourt. If historians were to relate everything that happened "I suppose that even the whole world would not have room for the books that would be written."[19] The historian must choose which of the billions of daily events she or he records and how they are interpreted. Even if we read accounts of the same event in, say, the *Daily Telegraph* and the *Guardian* we may sometimes conclude that the writers of each were at different events altogether. Even history is an art. So, therefore, there are differing accounts of exactly how David became King of Israel.

Despite the difficulties of the historian, biblical history at least presents factual accounts of events in the life of God's people. But some parts of the Bible are not history at all and should be received on the level intended by the author. The religious person, as opposed to the person of faith, will find this impossibly difficult. How confusing to realise that, while there is history in the Bible, some of it is story, or poetry, or philosophy.

Let us examine, for example, the book of Job. Job is a work of the deepest philosophy, an attempt to grapple with the problem of apparently undeserved suffering. There are 39 chapters of dialogue in poetic form in which Job debates with Eliphaz, Bildad and Zophar; then with Elihu and finally with God Himself. In order to give this poetic dialogue a frame, a prose introduction and epilogue have been added. In the prose God and the satan wager on the endurance of Job. As a test, in one day Job loses first his 500 yoke of oxen, his 500 donkeys and the servants who tended them; next he loses his 7,000 sheep and their shepherds; after that he loses his 3,000 camels and their keepers; finally he loses all his seven sons and three daughters. As if these losses were not sufficient, on another day Job is afflicted with sores all over his body. 39 chapters later, after his trials are over, Job manages to acquire 14,000 sheep, 6,000 camels, 1,000 yoke of oxen, 1,000 donkeys, another seven sons and three daughters of surpassing beauty, and he lived for another 140 years. Only the religious person could see this as anything other than a device to frame a profound philosophical treatise. And does this diminish the story? On the contrary, it enhances it, because we are dealing with extraordinary honesty with the deep "why?" questions of the world.

Then we may consider the little book of Jonah. Placed among the Minor Prophets, Jonah is quite unlike their work. In this little book Jonah runs away from God to sea, gets thrown overboard in a storm, swallowed by a fish and spewed up on the beach three days later for a second chance at preaching God's love to the Gentiles of Nineveh. Even a cursory reading in faith will discover that this little story is intended to reveal God's concern for the Gentiles and even for their animals: "Nineveh has more than a hundred and twenty thousand people who cannot tell their right hand from their left, and many cattle as well. Should I not be concerned about that great city?"[20] I suggest that, while we are debating whether or not Jonah really was swallowed by a fish and miraculously survived for three days under water, we are very conveniently avoiding the real but, for religious people, uncomfortable issue that God cares for those outside the community of faith. How dare He? And avoiding the even more uncomfortable fact that Jesus claimed Jonah was a prediction of His ministry and Passion.[21]

In fact so much of the debate about the literal truth of the Bible is a smokescreen, for while we discuss endlessly whether Jesus' "grandfather" on Joseph's side was called Heli[22] or Jacob[23] and, while those of a more catholic disposition reliably assert that His grandfather on Mary's side was called Joaquim we are conveniently sidestepping the awesome truth of the Incarnation.

It seems particularly obtuse to fail to recognise story and myth in Scripture when we consider that Jesus' characteristic teaching method was to tell stories. "A man was going down from Jerusalem to Jericho, when he fell into the hands of robbers ..."[24] Well, yes, that was probably a regular occurrence, but did a priest and a Levite *really* pass by on the other side? And did a hated Samaritan *really* stop and sort the man out? And how do we know the man was a Jew in any case? He may have been a Samaritan himself, except that it doesn't matter, he was a *man* and it's a *story*. Then again, "There was a man who had two sons. The younger one said to his father, 'Father, give me my share of the estate'. ..."[25] Well yes, but was this a *real* account? No, it was a story and a very unrealistic and seriously challenging and open-ended story at that.

The parables of Jesus are profoundly disquieting, in particular because they hide their meaning so thoroughly. With the possible exception of a few friends, Jesus steadfastly refused to explain his parables to anyone. You have to work it all out for yourself; and all we can say about parables with any certainty is this: If you think you know what they mean you're almost certainly wrong.

I used to speak regularly at primary school assemblies, and a very great privilege it was too. My preferred method was to use stories and, like Jesus, to leave the children to work out the meaning for themselves. However in one school I was greatly hampered in my work by the headteacher. Each week I would tell the children a parable, almost always a Gospel story, reworked so the children wouldn't think, "Bible story, yuk," and switch off. And every week the same thing happened. I would conclude with the usual enigmatic ending and then the head would stand up and say, "Thank you so much, Mr King, for your lovely story. Now children, what he meant was …" and so spoil the point of it all. There was one little flash of light though. One week a little boy came to me after assembly and said, "I like your stories. Do you make them up yourself?" And I was able to reply, "No, a friend of mine made them up, Jesus. And you'll find them, if you look, in the Bible.

Parables are supposed to get you thinking for years to come. There are some parables about which I have very little idea what the meaning is; the parable of the lost son[26] in particular has fascinated me for years. For years I thought of writing a novel based on the parable. It fascinated Henri Nouwen too, so much so that he did write a book about it, *The Return of the Prodigal Son.*[27] To help him, Nouwen went to St Petersburg and sat for a week in front of the Rembrandt painting of the same name. How apt that, looking for meaning, he should turn not to a commentary or treatise but to a work of art. Art, like parables themselves, can get to the deeper meaning and yet leaves more questions tantalisingly unanswered. Nouwen's poetic work has become a classic, treasured by thousands. And yet, as I am sure he would acknowledge himself, his work, though deep, leaves open as many questions as it answers. That is the way with parables.

WE may go further with story; faith itself is like a story. Which is more "real"? This? I boarded a suburban train, the 14.06 I think it was. It must have come from Dorking or Effingham Junction or Chessington South because it came into platform 1 at Raynes Park and the trains from Hampton Court, Kingston and Shepperton come into platform 2. It was a four-car suburban electric unit and I got into the front carriage. I sat down and I thought, "God loves me. That's nice." Or this? I met him on a train, I got on and there he was and we fell to talking. He looked – how can I put it? – odd. Shabby clothes and a northern accent; he wore a straggly beard and I could see, even though it was November, that he wore no socks; funny how you remember little things. Yet, for all that, there was a hint of the aristocrat about him too, and he seemed to know about lots of things; he should have been on *Mastermind*. We talked all the way to London and he was just, so interesting. We swapped phone numbers before we left and that's how I got to know him.

I didn't swap phone numbers with Jesus (Josh), what's His phone number anyway? But I did begin a life of prayer and for a person of faith the story seems to capture that faith far more pertinently than any statement of "verifiable" fact.

Stories are not necessarily "untrue", those are "tall stories", real stories are true on a more profound level. The Good Samaritan is a true story because it illustrates the truth about life itself. Jonah is a true story because God really does care for the people of Nineveh, and Baghdad, and Tehran and Riyadh, as well as the people of Virginia Water and Sevenoaks. My story is true because on that day I had an encounter with God in Jesus which can be verified in the changed life which resulted and results. And my poem is true because I do occasionally experience:

> "a flash or shiver,
> Quiver of light penetrating the gloom"

And as a result I take the plunge and dive into some act of radical trust. What about this?

———•◦•———

Disciple

What? Would you demand my soul, my all?
    My life friends, family,
Reputation, status to follow your call?
Would you have me carry a cross and give
    My time, money, home?
Ah! Yes you would, and more besides, that I might live.
For death to self, though God it hurts, is but a door
    Opening on eternity
Where love, joy and peace reside and still much more.
Giving all, I find I want no more than this:
    To gaze on Jesus' face,
To hear His call, do His will, and feel His kiss.
Loveliness engulfs my soul, the song of praise
    Raises from angels and
From saints I knew once as sinners with their selfish ways.
For heaven is free yet costs not less than everything
    And this is less than
Nothing. For Jesus' love I give it all, for He is King.

Poetry is not quite the same as story. But we may and must surmise that faith is poetry as well as story. In this poem I tell the story of a disciple; I wish I could honestly say it was my story. I could have written this:

The disciple should devote all her time, money and possessions to the service of God. It is not an easy decision. She must decide to religiously (that word again) dedicate the whole of life to God. For a while it feels good. But it certainly becomes a grind later on.

That's a bit like the Monty Python famous first drafts: "I strolled about by myself for a bit…" for "I wandered lonely as a cloud…"

The Bible has lots of wonderful poetry. Poetry never quite survives translation but even in English we can get the gist. Much of the work of Jeremiah, and of the unknown prophet we call Deutero-Isaiah[28] is poetry. But then there is the extraordinary book Song of Songs (or Song of Solomon). This erotic love poem was for many in the Middle Ages their favourite book of the Bible. John of the Cross knew it from memory and his spirituality is based on its erotic imagery.

Now, let's not be fooled. When the Song says this:

> How beautiful your sandaled feet,
> > O prince's daughter!
> Your graceful legs are like jewels,
> > The work of a craftsman's hands.
> Your navel is a rounded goblet
> > That never lacks blended wine.
> Your waist is a mound of wheat
> > Encircled by lilies.
> Your breasts ....[29]

STOP! This is unsuitable for wholesome family reading.

Make no mistake the lover in this passage is not sitting down to a chaste cup of tea with his beloved here. This is raunchy stuff. Dynamite. St John of the Cross equates the erotic imagery of the Song with our growth into union with God Himself.

> You looked with love upon me
> And deep within, your eyes imprinted grace;
> This mercy set me free,
> Held in your love's embrace,
> To lift my eyes adoring to your face.[30]

John, as you can see even in this fragment, was a great poet too; and wrote rather better poetry than prose because he related to God on the level of the heart.

The Song of Songs is rather neglected now. When my friend Paul Simpson, a leader of a House Fellowship, preached in my church recently I was surprised and delighted that he chose for his text the Song. I can't recall anyone else ever doing that. Could this be because religious people dare not think of God as a divine Lover, reaching out to possess the beloved who freely gives him- or herself to God? Could it be, though, that the Song is the pinnacle of the experience of faith?

You can't get much less religious than the Song of Songs. It is a direct confrontation with religion in all its forms. It proposes a life of "faith, hope and love. But the greatest of these is love;"[31] and goes even further than Paul's *agape* into the world of *eros*.

Religion is a curiously passionless occupation. True, religious people get worked up enough to fight wars, fly planes into tall buildings and set fire to one another, but there is a coldness in the extremism. It is a grim business, devoid of humour, devoid even of humanity. Religion lacks life. In Adrian Plass' *Sacred Diary* there is a character called Mr Lamberton-Pincney who runs a group in the church called "Spot it and Stop it"; Adrian explains, "They look for things to ban."[32]

On a more chilling note, in Philip Yancey's book *What's so Amazing About Grace?* the author, quoting from another of his books, *The Jesus I Never Knew*, tells a story related to him by a friend about a prostitute who had sunk so low she was renting out her two-year-old daughter for sex so she could support her drug habit.

> "At last I asked if she had ever thought of going to a church for help. I will never forget the look of pure, naïve shock that crossed her face. 'Church!' she cried. 'Why would I ever go there? I was already feeling terrible about myself. They'd just make me feel worse.'"[33]

That's religion she was afraid of, not faith.

I once began a talk at a Baptism service, for which the church was packed with those who do not normally come, like this:

> People often think Vicars must be terribly religious. Being a Vicar can be a bit like being the psychiatrist in *Fawlty Towers*, people think they have to be careful what they say. Sometimes people try to get in first by saying something like, 'I'm not

religious, you know', so they can go on swearing and finish their beer.

Goodness! If only they knew! I'm the least religious person I know. How could I be religious? I like football and beer and good food and sex and sensuality and holidays and theatre and opera. I like *Private Eye* and *Little Britain*. In fact the only really religious thing about me is that, like most Vicars, I also like trains. Religion doesn't turn me on. All those doctrines and creeds, all that respectability and pretence.

But you know what I'm really passionate about? Well, it's not 'what?' it's 'who?' I'm passionate about Jesus. And what's more He's the same about me. And that makes me passionate about life. That's what really gets me going. And it all started because one day I discovered for myself what we read just now in the Bible, 'If anyone is in Christ, he is a new creation; the old has gone, the new has come!'[34]

On a good day I am passionate about God. I aspire to make it true on every day because I long to be free of the religion that squashes the life out of its adherents; so that I can allow myself in company with all who long for God, in faith, to be drawn deeper into passionate union with God, the divine Lover who seeks intimacy with you as well as with me.

Endnotes

[11] *Joshua* Joseph Girzone (Prentice Hall and IBD 1987)
[12] 1 Corinthians 11:23. This is an earlier account than that in the Gospels
[13] 1 Corinthians 12:13
[14] Genesis 1:1-2:3 is the first account, the second and different account is Genesis 2:4-25
[15] Compare Genesis 1:24-27 and Genesis 2:18-20
[16] Genesis 1:27
[17] Genesis 2:21f

[18] 2 Samuel 2:4, 2 Samuel 5:3 and 1 Chronicles 11:3

[19] John 21:25

[20] Jonah 4:11

[21] Luke 11:29-32

[22] Luke 3:23

[23] Matthew 1:16

[24] Luke 10:30

[25] Luke 15:12

[26] Luke 15:11-32

[27] *The Return of the Prodigal Son* Henri Nouwen (DLT 1994)

[28] Isaiah 40-55

[29] Song 7:1-3

[30] *Canticle* John of the Cross (stanza 32) Translation by Marjorie Flower OCD in *The Impact of God* Iain Matthew (Hodder and Stoughton 1995) which is good an introduction to John as you'll find.

[31] 1 Corinthians 13:13

[32] *The sacred Diary of Adrian Plass (aged 37 ¾)* Adrian Plass (Marshall Pickering 1987 p 66)

[33] *What's so Amazing About Grace?* Philip Yancey (Zondervan 1997 p 11)

[34] 2 Corinthians 5:17

Chapter 3
FAITH AS MUSIC

CONSIDER a performance of a Beethoven Piano Concerto interrupted every now and again by the voice of a musicologist announcing, by number, the start of each new phrase. Yes, it really did happen, and on Radio 3. I suspect there were rather fewer, if any, listeners at the end of that particular programme than at the beginning. I also suspect that Beethoven himself would have been utterly unaware of the analysis and horrified by it. Two hundred years later, it is said, Béla Bartók was confronted by an eager student who enthused in great detail about the structure of one of his works. Eventually Bartók interrupted him with the chilling words, "If I'd known all that I would never have written it."

Excellence in music is often supposed to accompany excellence in mathematics and it may be so, but many if not most of the great composers did not sit down and work out their music like a mathematician, they conceived of it in one great thought. Bach could improvise on any theme at will; even Stravinsky, who generally worked out his music sitting at the piano, referring to his ballet *Le Sacre du Printemps* (The Rite of Spring), said he was "the vessel through which *Le Sacre* passed"[35].

MANY years ago, when I was an eager young music student, I and those similarly enthusiastic students with whom I shared a house would sit up late into the night arguing about the subtle differences in sound between one performer and another; we all had our favourites. Sometimes the discussions would become quite heated, but sooner or later we always ran up against the same brick wall. Using words, you cannot adequately describe a sound. What one person calls "focussed", another will say resembles a strangled cat.

It's like a discussion I had with my wife, she wanted the kitchen painted green and I wanted it blue. In some households the resulting compromise would involve going for green, but eventually we found the perfect (?) solution, we found a colour which she called blue and I called green; I couldn't imagine how she could call it blue, but that was the way she saw it, but we'd both made the sacrifice so that's all right. You cannot describe colour any better than you can sound. If you can communicate adequately with words, why use music or colour? If you can communicate in prose why write poetry? If you can rely on a creed why bother with faith, for we "live by faith not by sight."[36]

We musicians were, in the 1970s, involved in performing and listening to a lot of *avant-garde* music, known to some of us in the profession as "squeaky gate music". I once spent a summer in Venice making those sounds I had spent years learning *not* to make. A review of my solo performance in *Il Gazettino* referred to it as "stupendamente" which I took to mean stupendous, but I have wondered since whether it didn't mean stupid! Some of the cutting-edge composers with whom we worked in Venice that summer indulged themselves by writing enormously long notes describing their music in great detail. I used to think to myself, as we struggled to read the score, "If they can describe it in words why did they bother to write the music? "

———•◦•◦•———

I SUGGEST that, like music, faith cannot be adequately analysed nor captured in words, though gallons of ink have been consumed in the attempt, matched only by the gallons of blood, shed in the resulting fall-out. The earliest creed was simply, "Jesus is Lord"[37] which is plenty enough words. That worked pretty well for the Apostolic Church and even this seemed to be a bit of an add-on to earliest practice as the following story shows.

In Acts 8 we read about Philip and the Ethiopian eunuch. The eunuch was reading Isaiah 53 when Philip met him. Convinced by Philip's explanation of the Suffering Servant the eunuch asked, "'Look, here is water. Why shouldn't I be baptised?'"[38] Then the author goes on, "And he gave orders to stop the chariot. Then … Philip baptised him."[39] Unhappy with the immediacy of the baptism some later scribe inserted an extra verse, not in the most reliable manuscripts, which reads,

> Philip said, "If you believe with all your heart, you may." The eunuch answered, "I believe that Jesus Christ is the Son of God."[40]

It seems that even in the earliest history of the Church there was a tendency to want everything to fit into a neat formula. Before very long the Church had introduced more elaborate baptismal, and other, creeds which eventually developed into the so-called "Apostles'" Creed and the Nicene Creed. Composing creeds quickly became a bit of a habit; we have inherited, in the west and included in the Book of Common Prayer[41], the almost impenetrable Athanasian Creed, which has, incidentally, nothing to do with Athanasius; the reformers were keen to get in on the act too with their various confessions, the Augsburg Confession and the Westminster Confession among them. Even today the Evangelical Alliance, among others, has its own creedal basis of faith. These creeds, even the so-called Catholic (= universal) Creeds still provoke hard feeling, for example between the eastern and western Church remaining in dispute over the "filioque" clause.[42]

I confess that, when compiling a liturgy, I take every possible opportunity to omit the Creed or to substitute one of the simpler permitted alternatives. The only serious grounds for retaining a creed on a regular basis in public worship is as a hymn of praise. Which brings us back to music …

IMAGINE a court composer somewhere sitting down to write a movement for a symphony. His employer, the Prince, demands a new symphony for the royal banquet that very evening. Our friend checks his notes, "Thou shalt write a tune, then thou shalt write a contrasting tune; then thou shalt repeat both. After that thou shalt mess about a bit and change the key; but thou must finish with a repeat of the original two tunes and a convincing end in the original key." There are countless sublime movements written according to this formula (musicians call it "sonata form") by Mozart, Haydn, Beethoven and others. Sadly there were (and are) plenty of jobbing composers, like our mythical court musician, who pretty much followed the pattern by rote and their music is thankfully forgotten; they resemble the composers of jingles and inferior pop music today; when the session musicians in the studio have finished with a page they throw it on the floor, later someone with a broom comes and sweeps it up. The difference with Mozart is that Mozart dominated the form, while the others allowed the form to dominate them. A few composers, like Rossini for example, manage to stick closely to a formula and transcend it through sheer flair. But Mozart, like Bach before him, or most composers of merit, was perfectly prepared to adapt, develop, bend or even abandon the form to suit his needs. It is reminiscent of Jesus who said, "The Sabbath was made for man, not man for the Sabbath."[43] A little later Paul, musing on the place of the Law which had dominated his early life, wrote this,

> "Before faith came, we were held prisoners by the law, locked up until faith should be revealed. So the law was put in charge to lead us to Christ that we might be justified by faith. Now that faith has come, we are no longer under the supervision of the law."[44]

The Authorised Version has it, "The law was our schoolmaster…" It's as if the rules of form and harmony in music are useful for a promising student but the *maestro*, when she or he adheres to them at all, sits loose, driven by a greater law. Or to change the image: You can produce something that looks like art with a painting by numbers kit, but you'll never produce real art until you transcend it.

When I was a music student there was a movement which attempted to perform early music as it would have sounded in its own day. An iconoclastic colleague used to say, "Authentic? In other words is it played out of tune and with a bad sound?" Pioneers who played period instruments were expected to adhere religiously, that word again, to the instructions in contemporary manuals even when it meant the sound or intonation was not as good. I was quite enthusiastic about early music at the time and played in an early music group; the group was fortunate to get a lesson with a famous keyboard player. In early music the keyboard part is read from a sort of musical shorthand called "figured bass" which allows the player, if she can, to improvise. Our harpsichordist was playing away faithfully until in frustration the teacher elbowed him off the stool to show him how it should be done. "The only rule," he said, dashing off flamboyant flourishes, "is that it should be musical."

In the 19th Century so-called romantic composers were seeking freedom of expression; they were desperate to break away from what they saw as the tyranny of classical forms and harmony. But they ultimately found that in abandoning the classical forms they had invented new ones, in some cases just as strict as what went before. Those who are truly free, however, flourish despite the form, whatever its shade.

———————•◦•◦•◦•———————

MUSIC needs form; without it music meanders like the endless improvisations of a pianist in a cocktail lounge or hotel foyer. Composers who abandon an inherited form or shape in their music must replace it with something else, otherwise it would be virtually impossible to listen to. Nothing of meaning is without shape. Mozart, for example, never abandoned nor wanted to abandon musical form, unlike some of his contemporaries he simply transcended it.

Then there is a jazz musician who plays with absolute freedom, responding to the feelings of the moment, and yet who always stays within the structure and conventions of the music which make it possible for the musicians to play in harmony and follow each others' leads. Sometimes a jazz musician will break new ground and the other members of the band, being alert, will follow the lead. Jazz, like any other form of real music, is tightly disciplined and in the discipline performers find freedom.

Like Mozart, and like a jazz musician, Jesus did not abandon the Law, He simply transcended it.

> "I tell you the truth, until heaven and earth disappear, not the smallest letter, not the least stroke of a pen (AV "jot and tittle"), will by any means disappear from the law until everything is accomplished."[45]

This passage, which upholds the importance of Law, then concludes:

> "Unless your righteousness *surpasses* that of the Pharisees ... you will certainly not enter the kingdom of heaven."[46]

Then, according to Matthew, Jesus went on with a series of sayings in this form: "You have heard it said ... but I tell you..."[47]

The Sermon on the Mount, from which this all comes, is a new manifesto which affirms but transcends the Law. In it Jesus dominated the Law, the Law did not dominate Jesus. Like Mozart, He understood and appreciated the rules but He recognised their inability to produce righteousness, and He was prepared to break them when it suited Him, though always in obedience to the *higher* standard. Examples of Sabbath breaking, for example, can be found when Jesus' disciples plucked and ate ears of corn[48]; when Jesus healed a man with a withered hand,[49], and when He healed the man by the pool of Bethesda.[50] He also sat light to the failures of others, freely offering forgiveness to the woman who had been caught committing adultery[51] and welcoming without judgement all the unsavoury characters of the neighbourhood.[52]

In His approach to the Law Jesus seemed to distinguish between sins of *commission*, in other words what we have *done*, and the sins of *omission*, the sins we committed by failing to do what is required; He was much harder on the latter. Listen to Him addressing the Pharisees:

> Woe to you, Pharisees, because you give God a tenth of your
> mint, rue and all other kinds of garden herbs, but you neglect
> justice and the love of God. You should have practised the latter
> without leaving the former undone.[53]

The Pharisees were going beyond their religious duties, tithes of garden
herbs were not required; "works of supererogation" Roman Catholics
call them; but they were neglecting the basis of Law, which is justice
and the love of God. No wonder Jesus liked to quote Hosea 6:6, "I
require mercy not sacrifice."[54]

Rules work for the religious person, who equates to the jobbing
composer, but they are utterly inadequate for the person of faith. Rules
alone can produce neither music nor righteousness. Perhaps this is why
Jesus seemed to be so hard on religious people.

———————

THERE are two themes, perhaps like the first and second tunes in a
sonata, in what I have written so far: 1) Music cannot be expressed in
words and 2) the "rules" by which we create music are useful, but true
music requires that rules are transcended.

I want to explore these two themes a little more deeply in regard to
faith. In sonata form this equates to the "development" which I carica-
tured above as "messing about a bit and changing key".

The Christian faith is music. Firstly, and most immediately, it is something of enormous beauty which can be enjoyed and loved with little
knowledge of how it works. You can receive this beauty on a number
of levels. One of the many stories circulating about the maverick
conductor Sir Thomas Beecham is that he said, "The English do not
like music, but they like the sound it makes." This barbed comment
may be true, nevertheless music even when received on this level is
something of enormous beauty. You do not have to understand musical
form to love Mozart. But true music is an experience which transcends
the sounds produced, for the sounds are placed in certain combinations

and order. I am reminded of the wonderful appearance of André Previn on the *Morcambe and Wise Show*. Eric sat down at the piano and played a hideous cacophony of discordant notes. Previn said, "You're playing all the wrong notes." And Morcambe responded, "No, I'm playing all the right notes - in the wrong order I grant you." But when the pianist plays in a cocktail lounge it really doesn't much matter what he plays as long as he avoids obvious dissonance and it sounds mellifluous; this is not real music, it is aural wallpaper of the kind that spews out of hidden speakers in lifts. It is not intended to be listened to in any active way.

We could shift the analogy to art. When I was a very young child I discovered in my box of paints a shade of green which I thought was the best colour I had ever seen. In my enthusiasm I covered sheet after sheet with this gorgeous colour. It wasn't art, and that shade soon ran out, possibly before I had tired of it.

So-called Muzak can have its uses; I was grateful for it, for example, when riding on one of the narrow-gauge railways in northern Spain. As the little train rattled and swayed alarmingly over impossibly high and narrow viaducts they played soothing music to take the passengers' minds off the dreadful state of the track.

Music like this permeates your mind. If you find yourself whistling some aimless tune you may well have picked it up without even listening. Just so, Christianity can permeate society almost unseen through the prayer and holiness of people of faith within that society. It can even bring reassurance in times of anxiety. I would not have believed this possible had I not lived for a while in a culture which had not the benefit of a Christian inheritance.

But real music demands attention, it is not just pretty sounds, equating to my sickly green paint. Music engages the whole person, and deals in the great and eternal issues of heaven and hell. This is not always easy listening; it involves struggle too. There was plenty of struggle that summer in Venice, and not just trying to play chords on the bassoon, an instrument designed to play single notes. A young British composer was there, and while rehearsing a wind sextet with us, told us he had deliberately made the score unplayable as he wanted to convey a great sense of *angst* in the performance. Pieces like this do not immediately appeal to the "I don't know much about music but I know what I like" brigade. This is not the stuff the English "like the sound of". But then music is not all pretty tunes and facile eight-bar phrases. Music makes demands; music requires our attention; music expresses the darkness of the soul as well as the light. Like the great adventure inwards (see chapter 5) we encounter demons as well as angels in the eternal dance of music. This is not only the character of dissonant modern music; all music, like all art, involves conflict and tension as well as resolution. Music without discords is the music of the hotel foyer and lift. Mozart, among others, is quite capable of piling dissonance upon dissonance until you want to scream for it to stop, then at last he finally resolves the tension, but not necessarily quickly or easily.

Faith is similar. Faith is the engagement of the whole person with the reality of the spiritual realm. Jesus promised us glory, but He promised persecution along the way.[55] The way of faith is the way of a cross.[56] Jesus never promised an anodyne, sickly-sweet, dissonance-free life to anyone and He set an example Himself by suffering.

Faith, like music makes demands. It demands that you engage and allow yourself to be absorbed in its pain as well as its loveliness. A library full of words will never do justice to this faith, not the Apostles' Creed, not the Nicene Creed, not the Athanasian Creed, and certainly not the polemical Thirty-Nine Articles of Religion to be found in the Book of Common Prayer, nor even all of them combined. In the Church of England Ordinal (Ordination services) candidates are asked to affirm their allegiance to the faith revealed in the Holy Scriptures and "to which the historic formularies of the Church of England bear witness". This is a marvellous Anglican fudge but, I think, rather good. We do not have to subscribe to the Thirty-Nine Articles and few of us could with any integrity; so why do we encourage church members to recite week after week a Creed they probably don't fully understand and may not believe in its entirety even if they did? Why do we not, instead, simply allow the majesty of the music of faith to wash over us and absorb us into its harmony until we hardly know where the music starts and finishes, so all-embracing is it.

———•◆•———

IN traditional pictures of heaven angels are very often playing harps, or at least carting them around, which demonstrates perfectly well that heaven is like a spacecraft – no gravity. I once upset a colleague when preaching in his church by saying in my sermon that harps are rather effete. When I had finished he pointed out courteously, but firmly that he was indeed Welsh as I should have guessed from his name, Jones, and that he certainly did not think harps effete. But harps, trumpets, electric guitars or harmoniums, what does it matter? The point is that in listening to music we can become swept up in the timelessness of eternity. When you get "into" music time stands still. Until, that is, some idiot starts cheering almost before the last note has faded away; thus demonstrating both that he (and it almost always is "he") knew it had ended, and that he has remained firmly rooted in temporal reality throughout. The rest of us didn't want the music to end, and when it does, you want to be let back into the world of time gently.

The mysteries of the Christian faith are to do with eternity. Eternity is not an endless succession of days, that sounds rather more like hell than heaven, so perhaps the vile American website, which automatically calculates the number of days some dead person of whom the owners disapprove has been in hell[57], has some point to it. But eternity is not endless time it is the absence of time altogether, so that those who live in eternity are transported into another dimension.

Neither is eternity "Pie in the sky when you die." The Christian experiences, in some measure, eternity now, "A foretaste of the heavenly banquet"[58] as one post-communion prayer puts it. None of us has yet experienced the fullness of heaven, there is a "now and not yet" element to it, but the eternal magnificence of heaven is available as a foretaste and nothing symbolises it better than music. Listen to the great 17th Century Anglican poet George Herbert; in his poem *Church Music*:

Sweetest of sweets, I thank you: when displeasure
    Did through my body wound my mind,
You took me thence, and in your house of pleasure
    A dainty lodging me assign'd

Now I in you without a body move,
    Rising and falling in your wings:
We both together sweetly live and love,
    Yet say sometimes, *God help poor Kings.*

Comfort, I'll die; for if you post from me,
    Sure I shall do so, and much more:
But if I travel in your company,
    You know the way to heaven's door

"You know the way to heaven's door". Interestingly, when we try to speak of music in words we must resort to poetry. When we try to speak of eternity even poetry won't do and when we speak of the glorious majesty of God and the Christian faith we are more lost than ever; but music can give us a glimpse, a clue.

———◆•◆•◆———

THE Bible is full of music. The great Old Testament hero, David, was a musician (a harpist incidentally) which is not at all at odds with his standing as a great warrior. Music is not effete, it is tough, and tender, like faith, like God. I remember rehearsing a dreamy piece by Delius, it's called *A Walk to the Paradise Garden.* We were playing like a bunch of lounge lizards. In frustration the conductor, Vernon "Tod" Handley, threw down his baton and raising his voice declared, "You're playing like a bunch of wets. Delius used to hunt crocodiles from an open boat." Ernest Hemingway was, like Delius, another tough character who loved bull-fighting and big game hunting and deep sea fishing and hard drinking and hard living, who fought in the Spanish Civil War and wrote about it in *For Whom the Bell Tolls.*[59] But Hemingway was also exceedingly gentle, romantic and a practising Roman Catholic. He said that gentleness was an essential quality for true manhood. "When you least feel like it, be tender."[60] Why is the Bible full of music? Because music gets to the *heart* of the matter, like faith. It incorporates toughness and gentleness, concord and discord, tension and relaxation.

It is about the real life we cannot adequately describe in words. So no wonder we must "Speak to one another with psalms, hymns and spiritual songs. Sing and make music in your heart to the Lord."[61]

In some cultures all this would seem obvious, but in the post-enlightenment western world we have become so used to being dominated by our heads that we have almost forgotten that the heart and the gut have anything to do with our faith at all. Even as our world moves incredibly quickly into the less cerebral post-modern age, we still need to remind ourselves that our heads can grasp only part of the story. Music, the most abstract of art forms, speaks directly to our hearts, it stirs those parts of ourselves which "other art forms cannot reach". It connects with the deep place in our souls where we find God and true wholeness of being.

How do you join in? By picking up that harp, or if you prefer piano, violin, trombone, guitar or triangle and joining in. Or perhaps simply by raising your voice and adding it to the music of the heavenly choir. Or perhaps simply tuning in and allowing yourself to be transported by the celestial music which seems to play even in your own heart. By putting aside the grey temporal world in which we exist and allowing ourselves to be drawn by love into the great symphony of God.

———◆———

WE have spent many pages now on music as an icon of faith. Yet strangely they say that "when the devil gets into a church he does it through the choir." How could this be? Perhaps the devil knows what's really powerful in the life of faith, perhaps he is learning to speak the language of the soul too.

George Herbert regularly used to walk from his Parish of Bemerton to Salisbury Cathedral, a couple of miles away, to hear the choir. If his poem *Church Music* is anything to go by it must have been some choir. The day after I married my wife Monica we went to Choral Matins at Christ Church Cathedral, Oxford. Matins is not normally my service of choice, but we were both transported by the music, much of it by our favourite English composer, Henry Purcell. Rex Davis used to tell the story of how he took a Brazilian Pentecostal Bishop to Matins in Westminster Abbey and how the beauty of it had reduced him, the Bishop, to tears. It has that power, it is the language of the soul. We can have the same experiences with a worship band, guitars and drums; or with the gentle music of Taizé; or with Gregorian chant, now enjoying a surprise renaissance; or with a Gospel choir; or indeed by offering our voices to God in the activity we call singing in tongues. I was utterly transformed by the simple folksy music of the St Louis Jesuits, who in their profound simplicity opened my eyes to the reality of God's Kingdom. It is not the kind of music that matters; what matters is that our souls are attuned to the music of heaven, the language of faith.

When the Choir Master is more interested in his music than in the language of heaven we get religion; when the worship leader is more concerned with his image on stage than with the celestial tongue we get religion; when the Organist worships the instrument or the chorister his surplice or his position at the front we get religion. Musicians are a vain bunch, I should know, I am one. There are some serious egos in the music business. The famous conductor Sir Malcolm Sargeant, for example, was known almost universally as "Flash Harry".

Aware of these temptations to vanity "Tod" Handley used to say that orchestral conductors should be placed in a sort of sentry box, so they would be visible to the orchestra, but hidden from the audience, then they would be judged on the quality of the music not the meaningless antics on the rostrum. We should maybe ask why church musicians have been moved from the west gallery where they were unseen to the chancel where they wear strange robes and most definitely are seen. "Tod" also used to say that if we had really succeeded in a perform-ance people would go out saying, "What a wonderful piece of music," rather than, "What a wonderful performance." And when people leave church, if the musicians have succeeded people will say, "What a wonderful God." That is faith. Anything else is religion. Religion can offer a sort of music, the vain, precious self-serving kind. Faith alone can offer the music which "knows the way to heaven's door."

Endnotes

[35] Talk by the composer on the CBS recording of *Le Sacre du Printemps*

[36] 2 Corinthians 5:7

[37] 1 Corinthians 12:3

[38] Acts 8:36

[39] Acts 8:38

[40] Acts 8:37

[41] It appears under the title *Quicunque vult*

[42] This is the statement that the Holy Spirit proceeds from the father **and the Son** (filioque in Latin)

[43] Mark 2:27 and parallels

[44] Galatians 3:23-25

[45] Matthew 5:18

[46] Matthew 5:20 my italics

[47] Matthew 5:21-48

[48] Luke 6:1-5

[49] Luke 6:6-11

[50] John 5:1-15

[51] John 8:1-11

[52] Matthew 9:10-13 et al

[53] Luke 11:42

[54] Matthew 12:7

[55] Mark 10:30

[56] Matthew 16:24, 2 Corinthians 4:7-12

[57] I could direct you to it, but why should I encourage them by clocking up their visitor register?

[58] *Common Worship* (Church House Publishing 2000 p 297)

[59] *For Whom the Bell Tolls* Ernest Hemingway (Arrow 1994)

[60] *Papa Hemingway* AE Hotchner (Weidenfeld and Nicholson 1955)

[61] Ephesians 5:19

Chapter 4
FAITH AS DANCE

"O LORD our Lord,
　　　how majestic is your name in all the earth!

You have set your glory
　　　above the heavens.
From the lips of children and infants
　　　you have ordained praise
because of your enemies,
　　　to silence the foe and the avenger.

When I consider the heavens,
　　　the work of your fingers,
the moon and the stars,
　　　which you have set in place,
what is man that you are mindful of him …?"[62]

"Praise him with tambourine and dancing."[63]

"A time to weep and a time to laugh,
a time to mourn and a time to dance."[64]

"You turned my wailing into dancing."[65]

"'I am the Lord of the Dance', said He."[66]

WHEN the Psalmist wrote the glorious hymn to the creator we call Psalm 8, as with many others who ponder creation, he considered the moon and stars.

One of those golden memories: A summer's day in Bexhill-on-Sea, a day of sunshine, a day of walking on the beach, swimming, relaxing, enjoyment. The day draws to a close, we begin to feel hungry. There's a fish and chip shop near Cooden Beach; sitting on the beach in the quiet of evening we eat fresh fried fish and chips from the paper. The water laps almost inaudibly on the shingle, the sun slowly drops beneath the western sky, we lie on our backs on the sloping sands; as the sun sets, the moon rises, one by one the stars appear. A man rows his boat along the shore, we can see him in silhouette against the night sky. It's like music, we never want it to end.

City dwellers miss the night sky, the sodium glare of street lights obliterates its glory. When I lived in the Devon village of Cornworthy, worth a visit for its excellent pub, the *Hunter's Lodge,* as well as its lovely church and friendly people, the council asked the villagers if we would like street lights installed. I think almost everyone said, "No thank you." We loved our night sky, even if you could just see the faint neon glow of Torquay to the east, and one of my fondest memories is my walk up the steep village street to the church or village hall on dark nights. I never used a torch as it spoiled the darkness and it's surprising just how much light there is even on the darkest of nights. I loved evening visits to remote farmhouses too, sometimes it was so dark you could hardly see your own hand, but usually there was at least a glimpse of the stars.

When we gaze into the sky we are not looking at a static tableau but something in constant movement. Movement is life. Even inanimate objects are made up of billions of atoms and molecules all in a state of frenetic movement, even the particles within the atom are in constant movement. When movement stops we have reached the temperature of absolute zero and all energy and life ceases. In the sky the movement, though in fact very fast, appears as a slow graceful dance. The sun sinks, the moon rises, the stars which appear so static are in complex motion and "earth rolls onward into light"[67]. There is a rhythm to the universe, rhythm, movement, music, dance. And how very sensual that is.

When, in the 1960s, censorship was ended in the theatre and it was possible for the musical *Hair* to use full-frontal nudity on the stage for the first time, before that the actors, when nude, had to stand perfectly still, because movement and nudity together was, then, considered too sexy. Forty years later when nudity on stage is commonplace, and almost obligatory in Opera, I was grateful that a performance in London of a very dull Rameau opera was enlivened by movement, projected on the backdrop, in the dance and including several nude dancers. But we don't need nudity to be sensual, and it was the innovative movement not the nudity which relieved the tedium of the music. Movement itself is sensual; when Salome danced for the king, whether or not it was a striptease, it awakened his drunken lust with terrible consequences.[68] Could this be why religious people have always been deeply suspicious of dance, banning it altogether in many cases? Yet the smouldering passion of the tango, the urbanity of the waltz, the glorious fantasy of the ballet, the humour of Cotswold Morris (even if the composer Arnold Bax wrote that "one should try everything once, except incest and folk-dancing"[69]), the unifying fun of the Barn Dance all enhance life, for life is movement. This movement comprises the slow movement of culture which takes Centuries, the rhythm of life and death which takes a lifetime, the annual, monthly and weekly rhythms of our lives, the rhythm of music, walking, work and even the rhythm of sleep as we move in and out of the dreaming state; and for people of faith, the rhythm of prayer and our walk with God who is "Lord of the Dance".

> "I danced in the morning when the world was begun,
> and I danced in the moon and the stars and the sun,
> and I came down from heaven and I danced on the earth;
> at Bethlehem I had my birth:
> > *Dance, then wherever you may be;*
> > *I am the Lord of the Dance, said he,*
> > *and I'll lead you all, wherever you may be,*
> > *and I'll lead you all in the dance, said he.*"[70]

ENGLAND is blessed with thousands of glorious churches, ranging from the soaring majesty of Salisbury Cathedral, to the space and light of Liverpool RC Cathedral, to the rustic charm of a mediaeval country church like St Peter's Cornworthy in Devon. How they all differ; in fact you can't get a greater contrast than Liverpool's two Cathedrals, the one light and open, and surprisingly intimate, contrasting with the mysterious darkness of the other. All these churches are part of our heritage; some date from before the Norman invasion, and others from every period since. I wish, though, that photography had existed in the Middle Ages; photography would have shown to everyone how in every generation old churches have moved and adapted to express the faith of the community which meets in them; the changes have occurred in every generation except, usually, our own. The walls of village churches were once ablaze with gaudy paintings of Gospel scenes, or hell, or some other improving image. But when restorers tried to return the corbels in the roof of Exeter Cathedral to their former bright and colourful glory they were halted midway because they were using the wrong sort of paint. It mattered more to use the right sort of paint than to recapture the gaudiness of the original, so now the gorgeous brightness at one end of the nave fades to a nondescript drab at the other.

Some members of *English Heritage* don't understand heritage at all, they have taken a religious view of it. When I was young there was a popular children's game entitled Musical Statues; when the music stopped you had to remain utterly still; any movement and you were "out". Whatever their rhetoric the religious sort of heritage enthusiasts are trying to freeze our heritage like a musical statue, and preserve it in aspic. One of the glories of St David's Church, Ashprington in Devon, for example, is its wonderful carved oak furniture: pews, altar, lectern, pulpit, reredos, a gift of the owners of Sharpham House in the early 20th Century. As part of the restoration the mediaeval screen was removed and can now be seen in Exeter Museum where it belongs. Such radical change would never be permitted today. As a bizarre example of the opposite, Ashprington used to possess an almost unique 13th century silver-gilt chalice. Nearly all chalices which survive from before the Reformation are either tiny, since only the priest received the cup, or have been adapted during the Reformation to provide a larger cup for the people. The Ashprington chalice was already plenty large enough for the village congregation and I used it every week. It is a simple piece and in it there is history. When I showed a visiting American priest around the church he was utterly awestruck by this chalice which predates the voyage of Columbus by over two centuries. I was deeply saddened on a recent visit to the Parish to find that its wonderful treasure is now installed in a bank vault where it will never see the light of day. This is heritage?

Mediaeval Parish churches originally had straw-covered earth floors, convenient for digging up, so bodies could be buried beneath; they were devoid of seating; they had gauze in place of prohibitively expensive glass; they were a riot of colour; and they were used by the local people as a market, a meeting place or whenever some local event demanded a large building. Over time the earth floor was paved; glass, often coloured glass, replaced the muslin; pews were introduced, first private pews placed higgledy-piggledy then, in the 19th Century, in neat rows which grid-locked the nave; galleries were removed and choir stalls introduced as organs and robed choirs replaced the band; in many, Cromwell's men smashed images and broke the stone altars; screens came and went; for a while three-decker pulpits obscured the altar which stood first on the east wall, then lengthwise among the people, then back to the east again. The life of the English Parish church is like a slow motion dance in time – until now. Now, just try to remove those Victorian pews and see what happens.

I believe in tradition, in heritage, as a living continuum like faith. Some conservationists, though, are religious. Many of those like their religion to take the form of the Book of Common Prayer introduced in 1662 and remaining the only prayer book in the Church of England until 1928, though already over a Century out of date even in 1662.[71] Religion is static, the rigid rows of pews, unknown to Cranmer incidentally, effectively isolate worshippers from one another and, with the possible exception of kneeling and standing, prohibit any movement for the ordinary member of the congregation. The most religiously static service I ever attended was not in the Church of England, though, but on one of the Western Isles in Scotland. Martin and I were cycle-camping and arrived wearing our best clothes, which unfortunately were still rather dirty jeans. The well-attired congregation was already sitting perfectly still in long pews which afforded access only at one end. At the appointed time the minister, dressed in a forbidding black suit and tie, appeared in the pulpit where he remained for exactly sixty minutes. There were no musical instruments, no participation other than singing unaccompanied the metrical psalms; and the minister preached while looking at his watch so that at precisely 11.00 he could disappear to the adjoining chapel where a congregation was already waiting for a service in Gaelic. The congregation remained silent for a minute or two then, starting with the front pew, filed out of the door and through the churchyard to their homes, without exchanging a word, with each other or with us. This crocodile was the nearest they got to movement all morning. There were a great many of them, however.

But here is a story of even less movement than that. In the summer of 1983 I enjoyed a marvellous holiday with my young family in Connemara. Connemara is that magical part of County Galway where John O'Donohue lives, whose inspired books on Celtic Spirituality[72] have enlivened many a faith. The sun shone every day, so much so that our water supply dried up. We had only bicycles and the road past our little cottage saw at most five cars a day. From the window you could look across the valley to a little church. One day I walked down there. It turned out to be an Anglican church with a red door. There are precious few Anglicans in Connemara, they prefer their faith more "full-blooded", literally in fact, judging by the bleeding figures in the wayside shrines. Maybe there was some paint left over from one of them, so they gave it to the Anglicans for their church door. I pushed on the red door, surprised to find it was open, and stepped into an ecclesiastical version of Miss Havisham's boudoir. The church was all set up for Evensong, prayer books and Bible open, but everything was covered in a thick layer of dust, as if the clock had stopped forever at 6.30. At some time in the past the priest, it seemed, had arrived, probably from a distance, said Evensong, possibly alone, then left the church never to return; or perhaps he never arrived. Either way, no one bothered to tidy up, it stood frozen in time. I wonder what has happened to it now, 25 years later.

———◦●◦———

A FEW years ago I cycled alone from Helsinki into Arctic Norway. It was early July and even in southern Finland it never got properly dark, and as I crossed the Arctic Circle just north of Rovaniemi the days grew longer still until one night, in the little town of Muonio, I looked north and saw for the first time the midnight sun. You might think 24 hours of sunshine would be a glorious experience but I didn't find it so. Families were enjoying a Bar-B-Q in their gardens at 1.00 am, children were riding bikes and running around in the small hours. I had previously been to the Arctic in midwinter when it was dark all day, which was equally unsettling; what a curious rhythm of life. I found, especially after the exertion of cycling long distances, I needed the daily rhythm of sleep, and while you can sleep in daylight, everyone else seemed to be constantly awake. I spent one long night, for example, discussing the hard words of Jesus while my chance companion smoked; I have a photograph of the midnight sun with, in the foreground, the smoke of his cigarette curling upwards, as a memory of the occasion. Human beings need rhythm, daily rhythm, weekly rhythm, annual rhythms.

While it may seem rather religious, the Church Year provides a framework for rhythm. It is, of course, possible to interpret the year religiously and it is very much harder to make sense of it in the southern hemisphere, yet, used flexibly and wisely it offers human beings the sense of the changing seasons. The natural year possesses its own rhythm already, the seasons come and go, the moon waxes and wanes and with it the tides; and the Church Year is a natural accompaniment. When people reject formal religion they look for their own special days to mark the passing of time, so Mothering Sunday has become Mothers' Day, and to it has been added Fathers' Day, Grandparents' Day and so on, which is all a nice little earner for the greetings card industry; then Remembrance Day, or Armistice Day, is resuming an importance it had lost; Christmas Day has metamorphosed into a secular feast and the prevalent Advent Calendars have nothing to do with Advent; then there are the birthdays and anniversaries. People need ritual, ceremony and rhythm.

The body needs rhythm too, which is why I felt so disturbed in the land of the midnight sun, we need waking, sleeping, working, resting, playing; and the body will tend to find its own rhythm if none is forthcoming. Since we are so rhythmic, it's no wonder dance is important in almost all cultures. Dance is rhythm, dance is movement, it symbolises the energy and vitality we long for. It expresses our inner life, our joy, our sensuality, our aggression, our love, our nature as sociable beings, it can even tell stories. As the dancers in a formal dance weave in and out they could be the stars weaving their own dance in the night sky; as a carnival procession snakes its way along the street it could be the tale of our origins or our history.

IN the previous chapter I mentioned how sensitivity in music is not inconsistent with enormous toughness, citing the examples of David and Delius. We could do the same for dance. Unfortunately I have two left feet when it comes to dancing, but I once wanted to be able to dance. I had assumed, however, that dancing was something only women did. There was a TV commercial for Australian lager a few years ago, featuring Paul (*Crocodile Dundee*) Hogan. The Croc is at the ballet; on stage the *corps de ballet,* all women, are wearing tutus and shimmering around on points. Hogan comments, "We have dances like this back home, the Sheilas dance with each other while the men get stuck into the Amber Liquid." At this point a male dancer makes a dramatic entrance. "'s'truth, there's a bloke with no strides on." When I was very young (I hasten to reassure you – *very* young) I was heard to say that I wanted to be a girl so I could be a ballet dancer. Isn't it lucky that Billy Elliot broke through that one to make his dramatic entrance? In fact the dark setting of that lovely film highlights that, just as with music, dance is not synonymous with a limp handshake. The violent backdrop of Mrs Thatcher's assault on the coal miners is not the obvious setting for a film about a boy dancer, but it is a stroke of genius. Long before Billy Elliot, David, as well as being a musician, was a (perhaps enthusiastic amateur) dancer of great vigour. He "danced before the LORD with all his might."[73] Sadly Michal, one of David's wives, did not share his enthusiasm and berated David for making an exhibition of himself. David, though, would not accept the criticism as his loyalty to God came before his loyalty to Saul's daughter.

Dance does that, it loosens inhibitions, which is perhaps another reason why religious people are so suspicious of it. Many is the introvert who, on the dance floor becomes, in an instant, a wild and passionate creature, unconcerned with the opinion of others; you don't have to be a king to let it all hang out. Personally I am shy about taking the floor but when I have I usually cast care to the winds and discover a new liberated "me".

———•◦•———

LITURGICAL dance has a reputation for being a bit effete and, if we use it, we need to be careful not to make it precious. But in fact liturgy itself is, or should be, a dance, rhythmic movement, drama. You cannot fully take part in liturgy unless you are engaged in it; liturgy is a grand dance in which we are participants, not spectators. Many churches stage elaborate ceremonial, with robed servers, incense, processions, action, and more. It resembles the Temple in the days of King Uzziah.

> Above [the Lord] were seraphs, each with six wings … And they were calling to one another:
> 'Holy, holy, holy is the LORD Almighty;
> The whole earth is full of his glory.'
>
> At the sound of their voices the doorposts and thresholds shook and the temple was filled with smoke.[74]

Reading between the lines, Isaiah is in the Temple for some great festival. Imagine it, the carved seraphs with their gilt wings glittered in the firelight, the songs of the choirs tossed to and fro across the Temple, the trumpets and drums, the processions and the clouds of incense billowing all around all contributed to the sense of awe. This is liturgy at its best. It involves and draws the people in. As a result Isaiah has the profound meeting with God during which he was commissioned as a prophet.

In many churches there is similarly elaborate ceremony. The bell rings, the organ raises its many voices; the great processional cross, flanked by acolytes with their candles, leads the robed choir as they sing their introit; incense pours from a clanking "smoky handbag" and on a clear day you can still see the altar. The priest, clad in gorgeous embroidery, censes the altar and the thurifer censes the people accompanied by an angelic boat boy; there are candles galore, and the silver and gold glitter in their flickering light. This is just the start of a magnificent drama and it's perfectly wonderful; except in one aspect: tragically, like the audience at Drury Lane, the people are too often immobile spectators, trapped in their pews and unable to participate except by making a discreet sign of the cross or genuflecting and trooping up for communion at the relevant point. I remember taking a service in a church like this and my overwhelming impression as we processed up the central aisle was that no one was singing, let alone moving.

Liturgy is a participation sport. In a cerebral church we need to remember that. It is something we *do* – we *all* do. In churches some-what different to the one described above the worshippers often raise their hands to heaven, dance and move with the music; there is a band and the people join in to sing; they speak or sing in tongues; there is dance and possibly drama, powerpoint slides and film clips; there is ministry with the laying on of hands and an altar call; but curiously, though many of their songs include the words *We bow down,* there is a noticeable lack of bowing down in practice and the whole show can be offensively casual considering the fact that God is supposed to be present.

But as the elaborate dance of good liturgy - evangelical, charismatic or catholic, it matters not a whit - progresses, God joins in like the fool in a morris troop, weaving in and out of the dancers, creeping up behind us when we least expect him and, like a court jester, tapping us on the shoulder; and when we turn round He is gone, but we somehow know He was there. This is where we find God, for He is the Lord of the Dance. God is always moving, always doing something new, always surprising us, always appearing where He wasn't before. God is move-ment, God is the dance, in short God is life. If God stopped moving the universe would cease to be, for then God's life would be frozen at absolute zero. If we would know God we will find Him when we join in the eternal dance of heaven.

Endnotes

[62] Psalm 8:1-4

[63] Psalm 150:4

[64] Eccelsiastes 3:4

[65] Psalm 30:11

[66] *Lord of the Dance* Sydney Carter

[67] *The Day Thou Gavest* J Ellerton (Hymns Ancient and Modern, New Standard 1983)

[68] Mark 6:14-29

[69] *Farewell My Youth* Arnold Bax (1943)

[70] *Lord of the Dance* Sydney Carter - in Hymns Ancient and Modern, New Standard (Hymns A & M 1983)

[71] The first Book of Common Prayer was introduced in 1549 by Archbishop Cranmer, though revisions followed in 1552, 1559 and 1604. Liturgy, like life, is or ought to be in constant flux.

[72] Among them *Anam Cara* (Bantam 1997) and the poetry collection *Connemara Blues* (Transworld 2000)

[73] 2 Samuel 6:14.

[74] Isaiah 6:2f

Chapter 5
FAITH AS ADVENTURE

CUTHBERT clasped his cross in his left hand and with his right grabbed the hook just as it began its long ascent. Not for nothing had he spent four gruelling years at HHS (Holy Hero School). The crane rotated so that the long arm, like an accusing finger, turned to point towards the unfinished office block, our hero swinging precariously from the hook. With perfect timing he arched his back, seeming to fly through the air and simultaneously drawing his gun, he landed immaculately on his feet a foot from the unguarded edge. The evil villain, Murgatroyd, disappeared from view behind a pile of bricks but Cuthbert was too quick for him. Leaping ten feet into the air he landed on top of the pile and, cross in one hand, gun in the other, began to scan the unfinished roof. Just too late he saw the enemy as he leapt into the abyss, his futile shots ricocheted off the exposed steel girders. Cuthbert uttered a swift prayer to *Yahweh Sabaoth*, the Lord of Hosts, in whom victory is assured, then following his quarry over the edge leapt to his death and a glorious resurrection.

He sat back in his chair as the computer set up the next game for his resurrected alter-ego. And so it went on all afternoon. He lost track both of time and of the number of resurrections.

———•◦•———

SUCH is our thirst for adventure and for a (spurious) taste of danger. In these safety-conscious days we dare not risk real adventures or genuine danger; virtual (and risk-free) adventure has to suffice. But suppose we told another story:

———•◦•———

CUTHBERT clasped his holding cross in his left hand. He took a couple of deep breaths and prepared himself for entry into another world. His body began to relax as he put aside extraneous thoughts and focussed on the adventure which lay ahead.

After a while his head began to clear and, quite suddenly, he found himself in unexplored territory as if waking from a hazy dream to find glorious dappled sunshine streaming through the bedroom curtains. …

———•◦•———

MY sister, Polly Vacher, who had already completed a solo circumnavigation by the conventional route, recently attempted, at the age of 60, to fly her single-engined Piper Dakota aircraft alone round the world passing over North and South Poles. She nearly succeeded until, having flown over the North Pole, she was thwarted by unexpected headwinds in Antarctica which depleted her limited supply of fuel. The Argentine Air Force had to fly her enough *avgas* to enable her to return to South America; without such generosity presumably she, or at least her plane, would still be languishing in Antarctica. You can read the adventure in her book *Wings Around the World.*[75]

Polly's story shows how, even for those few willing to take genuine risks, the supply of adventures is pretty limited these days. In days gone by there were any number of adventures on offer, there were enormous blank spaces in the atlas and Everest had yet to be conquered. Abraham set off from his home in Ur, with his family and several thousand sheep, not knowing where he was going.[76] That's an adventure. Columbus set off westwards from Europe for India, trusting only his hunch and his ability to navigate by the stars. There must have been a day on that voyage when turning back was no longer an option, the supply of food and water would be insufficient for the return journey. That's an adventure. Similarly, in the 19th Century explorers set off into "darkest" Africa without maps and often woefully prepared, later adventurers set off to walk to the North and South Poles. In all these adventures many failed to return, though by the 20th Century failure was beginning to look like incompetence rather than bad luck; Amundsen said, "Adventures are just bad planning." Captain Scott may have begged to differ. Polly Vacher had satellite navigation and a telephone which though they don't eliminate danger altogether certainly diminish it. Seventy years before, in 1930, Francis Chichester flew his tiny plane across the Pacific trusting only to dead reckoning to pick out a minuscule island on which to land.

Bilbo Baggins, the Hobbit, in his comfortable and well stocked home observed that adventures are, "Nasty disturbing uncomfortable things! Make you late for dinner! I can't think what anybody sees in them."[77] Though nowadays many of us tend to agree with Bilbo and other Hobbits, we still love a good adventure story, and even the semblance of adventure itself. *The Hobbit* was a best-seller and theme parks with the word "adventure" in their titles abound, offering the sense of danger on their roller-coasters, though woe betide them if anyone actually does get hurt. *The Guardian* newspaper recently published a guide to adventures; but it turned out to be merely a guide to energetic package holidays, not what adventurers of the past would have recognised as genuine adventures; indeed the theatres of past adventures are the packaged holiday destinations of the 21st Century, even space and - who knows? - one day the moon. Perhaps, though, adventures are not extinct; perhaps we have simply chosen to become as staid as the Baggins family who "never had any adventures or did anything unexpected."[78] Perhaps we have substituted cheap thrills, which are to adventures as a Big Mac is to *Cordon Bleu*.

There would never have been a book, however, if Bilbo had not with some encouragement from Gandalf, bucked the trend and set out on a genuine adventure, one which made him very late for dinner indeed. Among adventure stories for very young children there was, some years ago, a creative series, the animated television programme *Mr Benn*. Every week Mr Benn would go to the costume shop. Once there he would try on a costume and experience appropriately exciting adventures, as a big game hunter, or American pioneer, or an explorer, according to the costume. Eventually, usually when things were getting pretty hairy, the shop assistant would appear to tell Mr Benn time was up and he would find himself back in the changing room; but he always brought a tangible memento of his adventure back with him, tangible enough to make you wonder if his adventure had been "real" after all. And of course his adventure *had* been rather more real than Alton Towers or Lara Croft. There was some talk of making a *Mr Benn* film for adults but it doesn't seem to have materialised, more's the pity; flights of fancy are not just for young children. Now that the entire world has been explored and mapped, now that gizmos take most of the uncertainty out of any adventures we might have, adults and children alike may still embark on the greatest adventure of all time without the need even to leave home.

DONALD Woods records how Steve Biko, under house arrest and having seldom left his home town, was amazingly well travelled in his mind and more than ordinarily knowledgeable about the world. He warned that "the most potent weapon in the hands of the oppressor is the mind of the oppressed"[79] and never allowed the oppressor to claim his mind. The caricature of a typical American tourist shows that leaving home is no guarantee that you will broaden your horizons at all. The ubiquitous and uniform Holiday Inns and Macdonald's have attempted to take the last remnants of adventure, and packaged holidays and tour guides have removed what remained of risk, from foreign travel.

My friend Charles, whom we met in chapter 1, knows about risk even though he lives in a space nine feet by seven. His room is furnished only with a steel bed with a thin mattress, a steel WC and basin; there is little natural light in the room, he usually leaves it for only four hours exercise a week, and will only leave it for good in order to die. You can see a room like it on the internet.[80] It is stiflingly hot in summer as his room is close to the tropics and there is no air-conditioning. Charles has a monochrome television and a few books, paper and pens; he has lived in this room, or one exactly like it, for many years. From the confines of this cell he embarks on extraordinary adventures of mind and spirit and records them in stories, cartoon strips, poems and elaborate drawings.

Now that physical adventures are mostly unavailable we can still go on the biggest adventure of all, we can begin to explore the vast "space" inside our own souls and set out on a pilgrimage of faith which may lead us to places we never imagined we should go. Like Dr Who's *Tardis* and like the wardrobe in *The Lion, the Witch and the Wardrobe*[81] this world is far bigger on the inside than on the outside, "there seem to be no limits to the possible growth of the human psyche in its fellowship with God"[82]. It is an unmapped world with no *satnav* or mobile phone network and as such exploring it is a risky business, it can transform your life; in it we discover sublime delights and unspeakable horrors. It is a world of adventure and discovery, a world in which no living person has set foot before, once you have entered it, like Columbus on the Atlantic, there is no turning back, or at least not to the previous state of innocence. The ultimate reward and goal of this adventure is not discovering India but meeting God Himself.

The existence of the inner world is challenged by atheist scientists, most recently and prominently by Richard Dawkins in *The God Delusion.*[83] However in order to maintain his argument Dawkins needs to rely on gratuitous insults of Carl Jung who was, if nothing else, an empirical scientist like Dawkins. He indulges in plenty more gratuitous and insulting attacks on reputable academics, which tends to undermine his own reputation rather more than it undermines theirs. Modern psychology, as Jung discovered, affirms the existence of an inner, or sub-conscious, world largely in harmony with the experience of men and women of prayer over thousands of years. In Morton Kelsey's classic *The Other Side of Silence* the author, drawing on the psychology of Jung, illustrates using a triangular shape of which only the tip is visible in the outer world[84]. The rest of the triangle lies on the "other side of silence", here is the place of adventures. We can open a door which will give access to the other world, of which more later.

Tragically the inner world denied by Dawkins is also rejected if not denied by many unadventurous church members. Many churches are full of "Hobbits" who, like all but one of the Baggins family, never do anything unexpected. Actually these churches are not full but half-empty or worse, but not as empty as the lives of their members. Indeed churches and their members often resist growth by stubbornly resisting change of any sort, eschewing risk and the adventure of life and praying only with unchanging and safe formulae which are centuries out of date. They become curators of rather dull museums, housed in glorious buildings which, though these buildings have for centuries changed in every generation, they guard and fossilise. It has always been a puzzle to me why someone should go to church, often "religiously", when they won't engage with the Jesus who calls us to adventures; and it has always puzzled me, when I look at church notice sheets, how in the church which is called to follow Jesus the best on offer is a jumble sale or coffee morning. In this attitude churches and their members are as good an argument against God as any advanced by an atheist. One MP was reputed to have said, "Hands off the Church of England, it's all that stands between us and God." The Christian God does, after all, invite us to push the boat out and have an adventure, the adventure of being a disciple of Jesus who said, "Follow me,"[85] who knows where? and who sent His disciples out with "nothing for the journey except a staff."[86] This same Jesus invited the rich man to give away all his possessions,[87] and warned that, for all the benefits accruing to the disciples there would also be persecution[88]. He said,

> "Foxes have holes and birds of the air have nests, but the Son of Man has nowhere to lay his head… No-one who puts his hand to the plough and looks back is fit for service in the kingdom of God"[89]

All this sounds like a call to adventure and adventure means RISK! The "Father of Faith" himself, as we saw, long before Jesus took amazing risks: "Abraham, when called to go … obeyed and went, even though he did not know where he was going."[90] And the adventure of faith which was possible in a physical sense for Abraham is also possible, even necessary, for us in a spiritual sense. Even so the faith which invites us to start the great journey of exploration within does often involve physical, material risk as well; like the rich young man we may be invited to experience freedom by ridding ourselves of the possessions and wealth, which possess and impoverish us, and trusting God to provide. That means giving money and time which we thought we couldn't afford, relinquishing the bogus concept of "security" in order to obey; nothing kills adventure more surely than the craving for "security"; and what a confidence trick that is. None of us has security. Everyone reading this may, before nightfall tomorrow, have suffered a heart attack or a road accident; they may have had their identity stolen and their bank accounts drained; they may have lost their jobs; they may have had their roofs stripped by a tornado or their houses flooded with filthy water. There is no security. Since there is no security it makes sense to forget about this illusive and fragile concept and make the most of an insecure world by being an adventurer and sucking the juice out of it.

One of my tutors, years ago, told me how, years before that (I guess this was before the Second World War), he had given away his books and possessions so that everything he owned could be packed in one tin trunk. Thus, he explained, he was ready to obey the Lord's call to go anywhere at a moments notice. He did, in fact, go to India.

In 1970 I lived for a while with the Suddick family in Mombasa while I attempted to teach Kenyans English and Maths in a mission school. While I was there Lyn Suddick gave birth to a second child and shortly afterwards she and Don and the children (their first child was two) moved from the city out to a little mission station in the bush where they lived in a small hut many dangerous miles from the comforts we usually expect and "need" with young children. Even though Lyn is a doctor that was risky. Faith sometimes involves risks and adventures like these. More often faith involves taking the risk of commitment, metaphorically putting your shirt on God. It involves being counted, being accountable. It involves risking the loss of friendships, promotion, reputation and, in some countries, freedom or even life itself. Perhaps most frightening in this goal-orientated age, adventure means risking failure.

But more than any of this faith starts with and constantly involves taking the risk of exploring the inner world, the world without maps or

navigation aids, the world from which there is no return to past innocence, of taking the risk of going deep into this world, knowing where,
or rather to whom, we are going but not how we get there and risking
en route encounters with any number of the demons as well as the
angels which lurk in the hidden recesses of the soul, risking the deep
dark tunnels of desolation as well as the mountain peaks of consolation. This is the adventure "Cuthbert" embarked on in the second story
earlier in this chapter. We shall try to discover where it led him.

Where religion is the antithesis of life, faith is the last remaining great
adventure. But where shall we find faith? Jesus invites His disciples to
a life of radical faith in the Sermon on the Mount[91]. Familiarity has
blunted the impact of this manifesto so that we can no longer grasp just
how radical its demands are. Jesus said:

> Do not worry, saying, "What shall we eat?" or, "What shall
> we drink?" or, "What shall we wear?" For the pagans run after
> these things, and your heavenly Father knows that you need
> them. But seek first his kingdom and his righteousness…[92]

I know a Christian church, presumably made up of disciples of Jesus
Christ, in which the members were unwilling to invest in mission even
though they had £100,000 in the bank because, they explained, they
may need it all for a rainy day. Security again. How is this having an
adventure by following the Jesus of the Sermon on the Mount? Thank
God this church discovered that risk was possible in suburbia and thus
embarked on the adventure of faith.

The church in the west has lost any sense of following the radical Jesus,
because we have failed to take the plunge into the inner world. We do
not take prayer seriously. A "wicked" friend who was once my spiritual
director used to say, "The clergy tell the people to pray, but not how to.
And do you know why? Because they don't know themselves."

An agnostic I know said he believed in supporting the church, because
even though he didn't believe in Jesus himself, the church helped to
maintain the *status quo*. If you take the Gospel seriously you might like

to read that again; you probably didn't believe it first time around, or perhaps you did, which makes it all the more tragic. The *status quo*, the established social order, the systems of privilege and status, the unjust economic order, the military might and the hostility to community of a western "democracy", this is what the church seeks to preserve? At least the Hobbits sought to maintain a just and peaceable existence! But whatever happened to the Gospel which promises preferential treatment for prostitutes in heaven?[93] Whatever happened to the Gospel in which the first shall be last and the last first?[94] Whatever happened to the Gospel in which it is harder for a camel to get through the eye of a needle than for a rich person to get into heaven[95] and the rich shall be sent away empty?[96] Whatever happened to the Gospel in which violence is to be met with peace?[97] Whatever happened to the church in which the members "shared everything they had"?[98] Do flabby western churches really think they are followers of Jesus Christ when they try to preserve the *status quo*? No wonder the church is disappearing in a haze of irrelevance and indifference and jumble sales. The *status quo* can look after itself very well for the time being, the rich are growing richer, the social order is more entrenched than it has been for decades, the economic order is less just than ever and warmongering and injustice is as much the habit of the powerful in protection of their interests as ever was; all without benefit of clergy or ecclesiastical structure. But the church is called not to the *status quo*, but to the adventure of faith and that adventure begins when we take the plunge and dive into the inner world.

The Diver (1)

The man before me in the queue
     Takes the steps two by two,
Biceps rippling in the light.
He flexes muscles, wiggles arse
(Admiring girlfriend's on the grass
Below). He takes a leap and arches into flight.

"A perfect dive," the watchers say.
        But something's wrong. On the way
Down, he topples over, just too far,
And with a mighty smack
Hits the water on his back.
Paramedics gather round. No more diving for today.

I sigh. I had been filled with dread.
I had been spared.
He dived, (I would have fled).
For all the pain he dared.
        And I did not.

The Diver (2)

Arms outstretched I fly
        Gracefully.
I arch and cut the water like a knife.
        And rise
And nonchalantly climb out to dry.
        In my dreams.

Reality is more humbling:
        With knocking knees and trembling hands
        I inch my way upward.
On all fours I edge along the board and hold
        I peer into the abyss
And slip
        And fall
And grab the board and hold
        And lose my hold
And, spread-eagling, kicking, screaming fall
Down, down, I thought I'd drown
        But somehow up again.

It wasn't graceful, neither brave
        But this at least I can say:
I felt the fear and did it anyway.

THE adventure begins when we move from the first poem to the second. There are two more poems in the series but the transition from first to second is what makes all the difference and determines whether we remain stuck on the treadmill or whether we begin the journey that leads to life. In Mostar, capital city of Herzegovina, there is an iconic bridge. Most people will remember pictures of the famous arched bridge in ruins, shelled to pieces by Croatian fire during the recent war. Mostar, still filled with ruins, is in fact a symbol of what happens when religion goes wrong. But the bridge linking the (Croatian) Christian and (Bosnian) Moslem halves of the city has been reconstructed as a symbol of reconciliation, which allows the young bloods of the city, members of the diving club, to show off their prowess by jumping from the apex into the swirling waters many feet below. At least some of them jump off. Others simply don their bathing trunks, climb over the railings and flex their muscles for a while so the tourists can take pictures of them. Eventually they climb back to safety. In spiritual terms these are the ones who never embark on the adventure of life.

Again, many years ago, my musician friend Martin, who is an idealistic man and his ideals for the clarinet involved perfection, though when it wasn't perfect it was often rather horrid, went for a lesson. On that occasion his teacher remarked, "That's all very well, Martin, but in this business you've got to turn up for rehearsals at 10 am and pay the mortgage." How we all guffawed with disdain. Later, when we were making a living (and paying the mortgage) as musicians we saw that there was some wisdom in these words, there will be good days and bad days, it won't be perfection but you can't ever allow your standards to slip below a certain professional level. As I grow older still I wonder whether there wasn't something heroic about the idealism which will take risks in the quest for perfection. Maybe in life it is all or nothing, Monte Carlo or bust. It certainly is with following Jesus. Jesus invites us to follow him, not to turn back; to take a risk with no guarantee.

That adventure begins when we plunge in to the inner world and meet there the Jesus of adventures. The Jesus we meet then sends us out to live radical lives, risking everything for Him. I am not saying that the transformation is instantaneous, it is never complete this side of eternity. Rather it is like the growth of a love relationship. We shall explore this in chapters 9 and 10.

Before we close this chapter we will return to our second story and see how it might continue. It never ends.

WE can't eavesdrop on Cuthbert's journey though. No one may trespass on this hallowed ground and no one may enter the inner world of another. We would have to rely on Cuthbert telling us his impressions as far as he was willing. Fortunately we don't need to rely on secondhand accounts of the fictional Cuthbert. This adventure is open and available for us for real. If you want to know the end of the story you'll have to explore your own inner world. But before you do, a word or two of warning:

- Your adventure will be real, that means risk.
- Do not embark on your adventure without asking for the guidance and protection of the Holy Spirit
- Do not imagine that you will be able to return to your previous state of innocence.
- You will encounter darkness (desolation) as well as light (consolation).
- On your adventure you may well be asked to take risks in the outer world when you return. These risks could engage any part of life.
- You will never be satisfied with life if you do not follow these promptings.

THE inner world is not reached through a wardrobe, but by pushing open the, normally locked, door into your hidden self, into the other side of silence. The first requirement, then, is to become deeply still. There are many different techniques for attaining a relaxed stillness while remaining alert but this is such a foreign concept in our mad world that we may need to rehearse them again. Many of these techniques are described, for example, in Anthony de Mello's classic *Sadhana*[99]. In this rushed and busy world our silence is often invaded by distractions which keep us firmly anchored in the outer world. The anxieties which give rise to distractions are endemic but will ultimately succumb if we persevere.

In order to achieve a state of stillness we will be wise to attend first to place, time and the body. Place is important. Ideally we need a special quiet place where we habitually pray, in which we can place pictures, icons, symbols, candles, and where we can burn incense or play soft music. This place should be warm and reasonably comfortable, but above all free from obvious distractions, the telephone, other people's conversations, or reminders of how much there is to do. Personally I prefer not to pray in a room with a computer or filing cabinets, I don't think computers or filing cabinets are evil, they just remind me that I haven't checked my emails or filed my bank statement. If possible it needs to be a place where you can sing and dance without the fear of being caught; silence itself is not the last word of prayer. I often sing or dance my prayers; I remember on one occasion singing and dancing praise to God in a church when two teenage girls walked in. Believe me, it is embarrassing; unless you are unbelievably thick-skinned you need a special place. For many people the luxury of a special room is not possible, maybe they can carve out a corner of a bedroom, or maybe they can go to the local church or, in summer, find a spot by a river or in a wood. It is true that you can and perhaps should pray anywhere, but special places do help when it's hard to pray.

Then time. The inner adventure takes time. We'll consider this in chapters 8 and 9, suffice to say you can't rush prayer. Set aside time every day; the best time, not the remnants of the day when you are too exhausted to concentrate on anything, least of all embark on an adventure. Limit your time too. Allow, as it were, Mr Benn's attendant to bring you home when time is up. You can set an alarm on your watch, and stick to it. Do not give up before you had intended. It is a commonplace for pastoral visiting that people often bring up the really important issue just as you're getting your coat. God is no different, He often brings out what's on His mind towards the end of our prayer time. If you finish early you'll never know. And getting into the inner world, sometimes so easily done, can take a lot of time. Archbishop Ramsey was reputed to have said, "I pray for five minutes a day but it takes me fifty-five minutes to get there." And, while we're discussing time, remember again that the inner adventure is not the work of a week or two, it is the journey of a lifetime. Be patient.

Then we will attend to the body. Human beings are all of a piece, what happens in our minds effects our bodies, anxiety will lead to body tensions; some carry these tensions in their jaw, others in their shoulders, forehead, buttocks or fists. However it is possible to reverse the current and, by inviting the body to be free of tension offering the mind a chance of stillness. Posture is, therefore, vital. Physiologically speaking you are unlikely to be able to remain relaxed and alert unless your back is straight. If you want to know what it should look like watch a baby who has just learnt to sit up; that baby will have perfect posture and while many adults will not be comfortable sitting on the floor we need to emulate that straight back. If you don't believe me try this: You are sitting curled up on a sofa watching the late evening news on TV. You are tired and the news is tedious and before long you are feeling drowsy. Try sitting up straight and you will almost certainly find that you quickly become alert without losing the relaxation. It doesn't matter if you keep your back straight on an upright chair, lying on the floor (beds are too relaxing) or using a prayer stool. Note I am not talking about a *prie-dieu* at which you must kneel up straight, but a low stool which sits above your ankles and allows you to sit back on your heels without squashing your feet. Desk chairs are available which enable you to adopt a similar posture while working at your computer; you could pray in one of these.

Having got your body straight without crossed legs or hunched back you can begin to attend to your mind and soul. Remember to invite the Holy Spirit to guide and protect your journey; remember too to express your desire to God, especially that deeper desire for God Himself.[100] Now there are any number of ways of growing deeply still. First there will be distractions. They are like water, you can't push them away and the harder you try the more they bubble up. Distractions may not be distractions at all, they may be God trying to get through with a megaphone so don't be too dismissive, have a good look at these thoughts before you attempt to dispel them. On the assumption that distractions are a hindrance it is well to imagine putting them into a suitcase for safekeeping, somewhere you know they are safe and where they may be unpacked again when this small stage of your journey is over. You may like to imagine entrusting your case to Jesus.

Sometimes distractions concern important practical matters. You may need to remember to ring the hospital or pay the gas bill. These are easily dealt with if you have a piece of paper and a pencil handy, jotted down they can be forgotten for the moment. Other times there may be an inexplicable nervousness in your mind and body which usually responds to good physical relaxation.

Now you are ready to begin your journey how might you go through the door and arrive at the other side of silence? Breathing is important. Try listening to your breathing without trying to change the rhythm, then sensing the breath, cool on the way in, warm on the way out; feeling the life giving air permeate your whole body. You will probably find that the rhythm of your breath does change all by itself. Then remember that, in both Hebrew and Greek, the word for breath or wind also means "spirit". Imagine you are breathing in God's life-giving Spirit, and breathing out your anxieties, tensions and distractions. If this works for you soon you will become very still indeed and perhaps experience a sudden shift in your perception. This is the movement mentioned above from a hazy dream to sudden awareness of a new world. If this doesn't work you might try some other method described in *Sadhana* or *The Other Side of Silence* or the book of your choice. Or you might use the *Jesus Prayer* (Lord Jesus Christ, Son of God, have mercy on me, a sinner) which, though it is not intended merely as a way into stillness, certainly achieves it for many people.[101] Or you can simply reiterate Samuel's prayer, "Speak (Lord) for your servant is listening."[102]

There are a host of ways of getting deeper in and journeying on, among them the vital business of praying with Scripture.[103] What is most important, however, is that you find your way of exploring the inner world and do it.

When we explore the inner world we become aware of how we may continue the adventure in the outer world. This may be disturbing and challenging. Examples of how the encounter in the inner world led to radical action in the outer world are found in many parts of the Bible. One obvious example is the call of Isaiah[104]. This is particularly poignant for me as it was through dreaming this event that I first received the call to ordained ministry which led to ordination seven years later. Dreams are another way to explore the inner world. Other examples of the inner encounter leading to outer action are the call of Samuel mentioned above, Peter's call to preach to the Gentiles,[105] and the mission of Paul and Barnabas.[106]

Before we close this chapter and move on to consider the playful and symbolic nature of faith we may remind ourselves that the adventure inwards is not for the faint-hearted and not to be embarked on capriciously but, like the adventure of marriage "reverently and responsibly".[107] But for those who take the plunge, life will not only be quite different and often very much harder but also on occasion magnificently glorious. Happy adventure.

Endnotes

[75] *Wings Around the World* Polly Vacher (Grub Street 2006)
[76] Hebrews 11:8
[77] *The Hobbit* JRR Tolkein (Puffin 1961 ed p 14)
[78] *Ibid* p 11
[79] Steve Biko's address to the inter-racial studies conference, 1971
[80] www.dc.state.fl.us/oth/vtour/index.html
[81] *The Lion, the Witch and the Wardrobe* C S Lewis (Collins 2001)
[82] *The Other Side of Silence* Morton Kelsey (SPCK 1977 p 139)
[83] *The God Delusion* Richard Dawkins (Bantam 2006)
[84] *ibid* p 144
[85] Mark 1:17 and parallels

[86] Mark 6:8 and parallels

[87] Mark 10:21 and parallels

[88] Mark 10:30 among other references

[89] Luke 9:58,62

[90] Hebrews 11:8

[91] Matthew 5-7

[92] Matthew 6:31-33

[93] Luke 7:36ff

[94] Mark 10:31 et al

[95] Mark 10:25 and parallels

[96] Luke 1:53

[97] Matthew 5:39

[98] Acts 4:32

[99] *Sadhana: A Way to God* (Bantam Doubleday Dell 1978)

[100] Psalm 42:1

[101] You can read about the Jesus Prayer in *The Way of a Pilgrim* Tr R M French (Triangle 1986) or *The Jesus Prayer* Simon Barrington-Ward (BRF 1996)

[102] 1 Samuel 3:9,10

[103] Among the many books which explore praying with Scripture is the excellent *Praying the Bible* Mariano Magrassi (Liturgical Press 1998)

[104] Isaiah 6:1-8

[105] Acts 10:9-23

[106] Acts 13:1-3

[107] Common Worship Marriage Service (Church House Publishing 2000)

Chapter 6
FAITH AS PLAY

A SMALL boy is playing in the garden. He has made a "tractor" out of a cotton reel, an elastic band, a candle stub and a matchstick, simple things. He has used his hands to construct an obstacle course to try out how far his tractor can go. He is utterly absorbed.

Meanwhile, next door, a little girl is sitting by the flower-bed, in her best dress. She is making mud pies and providing a feast for a host of imaginary creatures. Her dress is getting decidedly grubby, and she is equally absorbed.

Now the boy's mother comes into the garden, assesses the situation and says brusquely, "Come in, now, and do something worthwhile."

The girl's father also goes into their garden and says nothing, but rushes back into the house for the camera.

———◆———

WHEN I was younger I spent a fair amount of time looking for a hero. It was a hopeless quest; sooner or later I discovered that all my potential heroes had feet of clay. So Isambard Kingdom Brunel was cast aside, closely followed by Aldous Huxley, George Orwell and many others. Even after I met "Josh" I still looked for heroes, only now my heroes were people of faith, one was John Wesley.

Wesley is still my hero and remains so because I can now accept that the sometimes blatant faults of prominent and prophetic Christians do not necessarily diminish their legacy. David blotted his copybook with Bathsheba, Martin Luther King was not always faithful to his wife, and

Wesley was a lousy husband and father, but all of them made a huge difference to the world. Among Wesley's questionable beliefs was one about education: he believed young people should not be allowed to play; he is like the little boy's mother who insisted he should do something "worthwhile", like checking the stock market perhaps.

It reminds me of my time at a modest public school in Hertfordshire, especially the first few years. The day began at 7.15. "New governors", as the new boys were called, were required to be in the bathroom before the alarm bell finished ringing. From then on it was one thing after another, wash, dress, clean your "fagmaster's" shoes, fetch his shaving water, get to breakfast on time, go to chapel, lessons and lunch. After lunch there was a brief hiatus, for me often filled with orchestral rehearsals, before the stylised play of compulsory games, rugby in winter, cricket in summer, or a run. Then there were more lessons, supper, prep and bed. Permission was sometimes granted to stay up late, but only in order to work. Once a week there was a quiet time in which we were free to do as we chose, but someone would come to check it was an improving activity like, presumably, learning Latin vocabulary.

At a previous school chess was permitted during these times, and for this a few words were permitted, viz: "Check", "Checkmate" and "Your move". One boy was given detention for saying, "Your move mate."

Even in the few minutes available for leisure, new governors, in their role as "fags", had always to be available for errands to the "grubber" (shop). On the occasions one failed in some way, time had to be found to write out lists of important dates in perfect handwriting. Thus I knew that the Synod of Whitby took place in 664 but not what a synod was. As a music scholar I also had to squeeze in my piano and bassoon practice. No wonder John McCarthy, who also went to my school, thought of it as good preparation for his time as a hostage in Beirut; the regime was similar to a prison in which even basic decisions are taken out of your hands, there were even iron bars on the windows.

In my school there was a distinct feeling that play was not a good idea, unless it was the stylised play of the *playing* fields. The idea was reinforced by the pseudo-adult cool of peers as well as the regime. How misguided that is. Children and even teenagers learn through play. Play is what gives life colour, meaning. It is no mistake that we *play* music, we *play* football, we go to a *play*, but I am writing chiefly of the spontaneous playfulness which is natural for children and adults alike until it is ground out of them by the disdainful cool of the adolescent. When it comes to my school I am, of course, exaggerating. Some play was tolerated and there was leisure time at weekends and, as one got more senior, more options, taking part in so-called minor sports, for example, in my case sailing.

As a child I had been captivated by Arthur Ransome's *Swallows and Amazons*. My imagination was stimulated and I loved to play out adventures using whatever came to hand. Near my home there was a lovely walk along a rocky coast. There were large rock pools which looked for all the world like a living map of a vast inland sea; there were islands in this sea and little harbours. It didn't take much to sail these seas except imagination and the stick from an iced lolly which would do for a ship, and many was the daring voyage I made across the ocean. Before long I was sailing in real boats, learning in a 12 foot Dart One Design, a heavy tub with a single gaff-rigged sail, not unlike the craft Ransome described.

Play does not require elaborate kit, though. A ball and a couple of sweaters or a goal painted on a wall and you can play football; a bucket and spade and you can create Camelot in sand; an upturned kitchen table makes a wonderful pirate ship, and the stairs of our house became a double-decker bus. With only a group of friends you can play Cowboys and Indians, you don't even need a plastic gun or those coconut halves beloved of Monty Python. A few blocks of wood or a pile of stones and you can build a castle; my father and I once built an entire model village in a Swiss wood, using only the stones lying on the ground.

Play is not taking part in particular activities, it is a state of mind. If you want to learn how to play watch a puppy or a kitten with a ball of wool or a rubber ball. My spaniel is no longer a puppy, but she never loses an opportunity to bring me her ball in the hope I will play with her, if not she will make a game to play on her own. Dogs have the gift of living in the present moment, they are entirely focused. They also have the playful gift of living life to the fullest extent possible in the circumstances. There are two qualities always present in really holy people; they all have a great sense of humour, and they have a zest for life, living it to the full.

WHEN my children were young we decided as a family to donate our TV to the children's ward at the local hospital. We did it at the beginning of the summer half-term. Two long weeks stretched out ahead with no TV as comforter, instant baby-sitter or anaesthetist robbing us of sense. So we began a lengthy period without a TV. Almost overnight I noticed that the children seemed to be more alive. They spent more time out of doors, racing round on their bikes; they invented elaborate games to play together; they read books, or had them read to them; they told stories to each other and I made up stories for my daughter about the little dolls who inhabited her (home-made) dolls' house. Our home seemed to have a vitality previously missing. Fortunately computer games had yet to take off. Later, when we moved to the country, there were secret dens in the woods by the creek, and when it snowed giant snowballs to be made, sledges to be improvised and even an igloo to be built, which lingered long after the snow had melted.

I did not have to teach my children to play, all I had to do was remove the obstacles which discouraged it. Children, left to their own devices, are like puppies, they play naturally, they suck the juice out of life, they focus intently on the game in hand. They also have the advantage over puppies that they possess fertile imaginations. Children who "have everything", on the other hand, are often bored, discontented with their trips to Alton Towers or Orlando, their plasma-screen TVs, their gameboys, their electric racing cars, and all the other paraphernalia which clutter their bedrooms.

Genuine play, like genuine adventures, can be dangerous. I have a collection of impressive scars, one on my forehead from a game of Cowboys and Indians, another horseshoe shaped gash where my shin was stripped to the bone in a roller-skating accident, and my knees were continually grazed. While I never broke any bones, several of my friends did while playing at my house. Nowadays, though, you can't take risks. Some schools even insist on children wearing goggles when playing conkers. This gave rise to a glorious cartoon. In the picture two mothers are talking in the school playground. One is saying to the other, "My son has a nut allergy. I've told him to stay as far away from the headteacher as possible."

I HAVE already said how play brings people alive, children and adults too, we never get too old to play. It is the life-giving quality of play which makes it holy. Jesus said, "I have come that they may have life, and have it to the full."[108] The mission of Jesus can be summed up in this one sentence. Jesus came to bring life, eternal life, life now, not merely after death, life in abundance. "The Wages of sin is death, but the gift of God is eternal life in Christ Jesus our Lord."[109] Long before Jesus, Ezekiel had a vision. In his vision[110] a valley is filled with bones – "bones that were very dry". At God's command Ezekiel prophesies to the bones and as the breath of God blows on them they come gloriously alive. Sadly the church has too often tried to turn living people back into dry bones.

In the years preceding my meeting with "Josh" I had already come to believe the Gospel, at least in part. I already knew that indulgence and dissipation brought creeping death, while real life was to be found in Jesus. One thing held me back: I thought that once I had become a Christian I would have to become dull. It was hardly surprising since religious, as opposed to faithful, Christians have taken the best news in the world and made it boring; they have made worship dull and unattractive, sermons dry as dust, music slow and ponderous; at various times they have banned the theatre, banned dancing, banned make-up and bright coloured clothes, banned pretty much anything which is fun. Religion does that. If it's fun and we enjoy it, we suppose, it can't be God's will. So worship became worthy but dull, and the Victorians built their railway stations like cathedrals but their churches like railway stations, especially their non-conformist chapels.

———————•·•·•———————

KEITH and Miranda are looking for the meaning of life. They decide to take their young family to church. We can only hope they chose a church with a bit of zest. Unfortunately not, and we will steal here a magnificent description of the service they probably went to from Nick Hornby. In Hornby's account Kate, the narrator, is taking her daughter, Molly, to church:

> The sparsity of the congregation, and its apparent lack of interest in anything or anyone, allows us to sit towards the back… Molly is of course the youngest person in the pews on this side of the church, but I am probably the second youngest, by ten or fifteen years… There is a reading, and then there are notices. They're having a bring-and-buy sale… It all feels a long way from God… It feels sad, exhausted, defeated; this may have been God's house once, you want to tell the handful of people here, but He's clearly moved, shut up shop, gone to a place where there's more demand for that sort of thing.[111]

Hornby is a far from sympathetic commentator. You feel he would love it to be otherwise, he simply records what he sees. He even introduces a Vicar who at least makes a misguided attempt at play by singing in the pulpit, until the lifelessness of the environment squashes it flatter than a pancake. You cannot command genuine play in church any more than Miss Havisham could command Pip to play in *Great Expectations*. Play is a spontaneous expression of life.

How can it have got to this? Playfulness is innate, but we have allowed the dead hand of religion to murder the playfulness of faith. Churches should be alive, that means they should be playful places. This in no way denies the solemnity of our meeting with God Himself - God is playful. The Wisdom literature in the Old Testament[112] introduces a sea creature called Leviathan, God's plaything. "There the ships go to and fro, and the leviathan, which you formed to frolic there."[113]

It is a big mistake to imagine that solemnity demands earnestness; play can be extremely solemn, even grave, though laughter is never far away, but it takes from our gravity the pompous self-importance of religion. Mr Bumble, Uncle Pumblechook, pillars of the church both, and a host of other Dickens characters enable Dickens to lampoon self-importance mercilessly – and rightly, it is a profoundly unattractive quality.

<hr>

SADLY earnestness and pomposity can creep into even games, frivolous games too. My flat-mate Julian and I, for example, at one time liked nothing better on a Sunday afternoon than to wander into Kensington Gardens and fly a kite. But it was more than our life was worth to allow our little plastic contraption to stray too near the "professionals". More than once we were warned off with a string of technical jargon incomprehensible to us. This is as nothing alongside the grim and joyless money-driven determination of professional sportsmen and sportswomen. "Some people think football is a matter of life and death… I can assure them it is much more serious than that." So said Bill Shankly, one-time manager of Liverpool Football Club, on BBC TV. But Boris Becker, interviewed after a defeat on court, put his earnest interviewer to rights and the defeat into perspective by saying, "I lost a game of tennis. So what?" Yet many the manager who now has to remind his players to enjoy their *game*.

It is a privilege to make a living doing what most people do simply for fun, music for example. There are certain professional standards required and seriousness demanded, but the professional must never forget that the word "amateur" is derived from the Latin word for love. As one musician remarked, "The day it's just another concert is the day I quit." One double bass player in the Sydney Opera, no doubt with these words ringing in his ears, held his retirement party outside by the harbour. When his guests arrived they found he had rigged up his double bass with a sail and as the party got going they watched it sail away. What a playful thing to do.

I MENTIONED that humour is the invariable mark of holy people, and closely associated with play; I mean, of course, the light-hearted, self-deprecating humour that laughs *with,* not *at,* others. One of the funniest books of recent times is *The Sacred Diary of Adrian Plass (aged 37 ¾)* by Adrian Plass. It obviously struck a chord because it remained top of the best-seller lists for ages. Not everyone was amused though, some disgruntled readers even wrote to the church press to complain of its lack of earnestness. It is not difficult to take the temperature of a church from the pulpit; the temperature is determined not by attentiveness, though that is a good sign, but by the readiness to laugh. I know that when I can't raise even a titter, I am in trouble. Naturally a preacher would not attempt humour on Good Friday, though Sydney Carter got pretty close to it with the verse,

> I danced on a Friday when the sky grew black
> It's hard to dance with the devil on your back,[114]

Incidentally one of the really good things about our school was that we got Sydney Carter to come and give a talk. We also got Marian Montgomery, Humphrey Lyttelton and Elkie Brookes to give concerts, so it was not all bad. Elkie Brookes even sang a song entitled *Big Bad Bill* which ended with the words, "Sweet William now." Poor woman, she was unaware that the head's name was Bill, and completely perplexed when the entire audience fell about laughing.

Plass' fictional diary is funny because it spots the absurdities of our church life so accurately (perhaps this is why it offended some people) and laughs with our absurdity not at it, this includes the author laughing at himself. There is not a hint of malice anywhere in it. We humans are absurd. I have a file of reviews from my time as a professional musician. My favourite is a review of an Elysian Wind Quintet concert given in London when Martin was living in Sweden, I was living in

Teheran and the others were living in London. The reviewer wrote, "With members living as far apart of Sweden, Teheran and London the Elysian Wind Quintet must have trouble getting together – they had the same trouble in the Purcell Room last night." I like that because it exposed the absurdity of our lives, it offered a critique without malice and above all because it's funny. I prefer it by far to other glowing but earnest reviews, even if I take a certain pompous pride in some of those. I am absurd, and humour can puncture my absurd pomposity and self-importance.

———•◦•———

HUMOUR often accompanies struggle. I recently heard Clive Stafford-Smith speak. Stafford-Smith is an Anglo-American lawyer, based in Louisiana, who defends those accused of capital murder and, most recently, those imprisoned without charge in Guantanamo Bay. He deals with terrible suffering and endures quite a bit of threatening behaviour himself, he was once threatened with imprisonment on the (false) charge that he had smuggled some Speedo underpants to a prisoner. His response was to produce a line in orange underpants (orange is the colour of prison clothes) with the words, "Fair trial, my arse" and the logo of his organisation, *Reprieve*, on the back. These were sold to raise money for the cause. As he spoke we were taken to some of the darkest places on earth, but there was a great deal of laughter too. It is a powerful weapon in the fight against tyranny; tyrants loathe laughter, they take themselves so terribly seriously.

God's people should laugh like this. The community of God's people is founded on laughter and struggle; two of the Patriarchs' names bear this out: Isaac means laughter and Israel means "he struggled with God." No wonder the Jews have survived appalling trials with laughter, laughter is a hallmark of the Jews. It is still ingrained in their tradition; many of us, for example, eagerly await the contributions of Rabbi Lionel Blue to *Thought for the Day* on Monday mornings on the Radio 4 news programme *Today*; Blue can even make John Humphrys laugh!

How sad then that many Christians, who also claim descent from Isaac and Israel, have forgotten how to laugh. Could it be because we have forgotten how to struggle as well as live?

—•◆•—

SOME people think we should be *deadly* serious about religion. Perhaps they think Scripture is devoid of humour. Part of the problem with humour is that, like faith itself, it is culturally conditioned. Humour does not travel well, we English even find difficulty in laughing at American humour, let alone German. That is why we don't laugh with the Bible. Perhaps we might begin by looking at the enigmatic little book of Ecclesiastes

> I commend the enjoyment of life, because nothing is better for a man under the sun than to eat and drink and be glad. Go, eat your food with gladness, and drink your wine with a joyful heart. [115]

The whole book is delightfully tongue in cheek, not at all the cynical treatise it would appear to be to a cynical person.

> There is a time to weep and a time to laugh,
> A time to mourn and a time to dance,[116]

Jesus, too, had a "wicked" sense of humour; He was, after all, a Jew descended from Isaac. If we can't see it we have, perhaps, become over-familiar with His stories, or conditioned to earnestness.

> Why do you look at the speck of sawdust in your brother's eye and pay no attention to the plank in your own eye? ... No one lights a lamp and hides it in a jar or puts it under a bed ...which of you fathers, if your son asks for a fish, will give him a snake instead?[117]

Imagine your favourite stand-up comedian using those lines and you might get the idea.

And for zest: Jesus is your man, He was the life and soul of every party and broke up every funeral including His own.

———◆•◆———

WHEN my children were young, every winter when it snowed we would go to the park where there was a wonderful slope for sledging. One day I noticed the local undertaker and the superintendent of the crematorium, dressed in woolly scarves and hats, whizzing down the slope together on a sledge, for all the world like two schoolboys; and I thought, "There is life after death, after all." Thank God for life and laughter, thank God

———◆•◆———

Endnotes

[108] John 10:10
[109] Romans 6:23
[110] Ezekiel 37:1-14
[111] *How to be Good* Nick Hornby (Viking 2001 pp186f)
[112] The Wisdom literature includes the poetry, philosophy and songs found in the books: Job, Psalms, Proverbs, Ecclesiastes and Song of Songs
[113] Psalm 104:26
[114] *Lord of the Dance* Sydney Carter
[115] Ecclesiastes 8:15; 9:7
[116] Ecclesiastes 3:4
[117] Matthew 7:3; Luke 8:16; 11:11

Chapter 7
FAITH AS MYSTERY

IN the autumn of 1973 the Elysian Wind Quintet toured the West Country playing on successive nights at a series of small town music clubs. One afternoon we arrived at Honiton station where we were picked up and transported by minibus to Ottery St Mary. It was a great concert that night; the school hall was packed with 300 enthusiastic music lovers and we rose to the occasion. Chamber music is the "music of friends" and playing in the Quintet I felt I was in heaven. But we've "done" music and it is not for the music that I remember our visit to Ottery St Mary.

The Ottery Music Society had arranged to put us up in a country house hotel, where a good dinner was waiting for us after the concert and, no doubt, there was a drop or two of wine to accompany it before retiring to our rooms. I slept deeply but remember that stay for a divine awakening. The window of our room faced east and outside was a huge beech tree arrayed in autumn gold. As I woke I gradually became aware of glorious dappled sunlight, filtered through the leaves of the tree, and I felt the most perfect sense of well-being. This feeling lasted for, who knows? A minute? An hour? I will never know, it was eternal.

That's my story. Not much to it. Or rather there is everything to it. It was an experience of the mystery of God, though I wouldn't have identified it as such at the time, being, so I thought, a non-believer. Later I was reassured to find that John O'Donohue had experienced something similar:

> "There is a lovely, disconcerting moment between sleep and awakening. You have only half-emerged from sleep and for a few seconds you do not know where you are or what you are.

You are lost between worlds… Such disturbances awaken us to the mystery of thereness that we call presence."[118]

Sister Macrina Wiederkehr describes something similar to my tree but in more detail:

"It is just dawn. Standing still for a moment, I see the first rays of sunlight shimmering through a silver maple tree. It is truly a moment of wonder, resplendent with light. I stand gazing as one in the midst of a vision. Suddenly I am uncertain whether those golden arms swaying in the morning sunlight are tree branches or angel wings…

"And then in a twinkling I'm certain. I am standing before a tree full of angels dazzling me with their glorious presence."[119]

I once saw the angels, in the spring of 1985. I was a newly-ordained Deacon serving in the parish of St Michael and *All Angels*. I used to go into the parish church in the afternoons to pray, the church was heated and it enabled me to get some quiet, away from the Curate's two-bedroom house which I shared with a wife and two very young children. One afternoon as I prayed, quite unexpectedly I became aware that the barrel-vaulted nave of the church was awash with angels. I wasn't aware of the form of the heavenly creatures, it was more like a movement in the light. Later I came across an uncannily similar description by CS Lewis, who introduced beings he called *Eldila* in his science fiction novel *Out of the Silent Planet*. "Sometimes you can mistake them for a sunbeam or even a moving of the leaves."[120] The hero, Ransom, cannot at first see these heavenly creatures, but as his way of seeing changes he becomes aware of them.

He perceived, gradually, that the place was full of *eldila*… He became conscious that the air above him was full of a far greater complexity of light than the sunrise could explain, and light of a different kind, *eldil*-light.[121]

My vision lasted but an instant and was gone. I had never experienced anything like it before, nor have I since, and I was quite overcome.

I was young and even more inexperienced then and made the mistake of referring to it in my sermon at Evensong. Someone in the congregation was so offended by my account that they set the local press on to me. The next morning, my day off, I was startled by an early morning ring on the doorbell and found, on the doorstep, a reporter from the local rag. "We hear you've been seeing things."

I don't know who tipped her off, though I had a hunch. If you were the one and can remember it and you're reading this, why not get in touch? All is forgiven. In the event I invited the reporter into my tiny study where we discussed different world-views and she soon made her apologies and left – without a story. It's not all roses working for a local paper.

I tell these very personal stories in the hope that they may strike a chord with you, the reader. Research has shown[122] that the vast majority of people, religious and non-religious, believers and non-believers, have experiences like mine, though often dismiss them or keep them to themselves. Gerard Hughes recounts one such as told to him by a young Scotsman.

> "Ah wis in Wales … D'ye know whit ah found masel' doing'? Walkin' the bloody moors wi' a wee dug... Ah came tae cliffs by the sea and jist sat there. The sea looked affie big and ah felt very wee, but ah wis happy. Daft, isn't it? Ah cannie tell ma mates, 'cos they'd think ah wis kinky."[123]

Some years ago I was accosted by a woman I recognised but had never visited. "Oi," she called, that at least was the gist of her greeting. "My husband's in hospital and wants to see you."

A conscientious priest doesn't let the grass grow under his feet after an invitation like that, so the same afternoon I drove to the hospital and visited her husband. He was quite ill but he didn't want to talk about his illness, he wanted to tell me about an experience of God he'd had many years previously, but had never dared tell anyone, probably because, like the Scotsman, he feared people would think him crazy. I was able to reassure him that similar experiences are enjoyed by many others and the upshot of it all was that a year or so later he got confirmed and joined the church.[124]

These stories are all accounts of the fickle touch of the mystery we call God. God is indeed like a jester, creeping up behind us when we least expect Him. Most people have these experiences. Some write them off as chemical activity in the brain, you can't get much more prosaic than that, or a hallucination, an illusion or something worse. Others receive them as the touch of the divine. The mystery is there, if you will only receive it.

Some, as I have said, prefer life without mystery and do everything to explain it away. Life is much safer that way. So much more secure to discount experiences of the numinous, and among them miracles,

———— •·◆·• ————

THE joke is told about some nuns who were driving along a country road when their car ran out of petrol. One of their number walked to the filling station but had no container for the petrol. The filling station could lend her only an old chamber pot, and when she arrived back at the car her sisters started to pour the contents into the fuel tank. Meanwhile a passing motorist stopped, jumped out of his car and exclaimed, "I don't agree with your religion, but I admire your faith."

Next day a priest was driving along the same road with his atheist friend when their windscreen shattered. Fortunately the part of the screen in front of the driver remained intact and the priest could see to draw safely to a stop. They were quite unhurt, and settled down by the roadside to wait for the breakdown crew. While the AA man was at work the priest was busy thanking God for the miracle of preserving exactly that part of the screen through which he could see the road, while his atheist friend was keeping an eye on the repair man to ensure he fitted the new windscreen with the toughened part in front of the driver.

If we take these tall stories at face value we see that in both stories one character perceived a miracle, while the others didn't. In both the apparent miracle had a perfectly rational explanation.

It doesn't help the cause of the supernatural if we naïvely accept any coincidence as a miracle, though it seems churlish to assume that God cannot work through ordinary means as well as supernatural, and at least part of a miracle is a way of seeing.

But what about genuine miracles? CS Lewis showed that before we look for evidence we need to decide whether or not we believe they are at least theoretically possible. "What we learn from experience depends on the kind of philosophy we bring to experience... The philosophical question must therefore come first."[125] If we have decided that miracles don't or can't happen then we will always find a way to explain them away; we could, for example, describe them as a conjuring trick.

There was a teacher at my preparatory school, for example, I can't remember his name nor the main subject he taught, but I know the poor man had also to teach religious instruction. He was probably a scientist, he looked like a caricature of one, unruly hair, thick glasses and great big staring eyes, but there was also something of the thespian in him, as you will see. In the lesson I remember, he was trying to teach us the story of Elijah and his contest with the priests of Baal on Mount Carmel.[126] He did a good job because I never forgot the story, though I may be remembering it for unorthodox reasons. Many a preacher must long to communicate as well as he did. He was a dramatic story teller and as the story unfolded I felt I was there on the mountain with Elijah. Then he got to the really dramatic bit: "And," those intense eyes seemed to be looking straight at me, "it wasn't water he poured on the sacrifice. Do you know what it was?" it was a rhetorical question, "Oil!" those great eyes lit up triumphantly. "Then," he went on after a dramatic pause, "Elijah stood behind the altar and" – he made a gesture as if striking a match – "up it went." I almost felt like applauding. That was about 45 years ago. It's a pity I can't remember what he taught me about science or French or whatever it was he taught. On reflection, though, he probably wasn't a scientist because he left a lot of unanswered questions: Did the priests of Baal not smell the oil? Where did the oil come from? How did Elijah manage to ignite it without the aid of safety matches and without becoming a burnt offering himself?

My teacher was describing a deliberate device to mislead the watchers by illusion. Magicians, conjurors, are often wonderful entertainers, I have myself employed one or two for children's birthday parties, and the best of them have taken their art to (literally) incredible heights. "How did he do that?" we gasp; but though they maintain the illusion of magic and never tell how they did it, they know, as we know, that it is all sleight of hand. They deal in mystery, but we know that the mystery has an explanation. Supposing my teacher was right about the oil, and the priests of Baal had been gullible enough to fall for it, which cost them their lives, even so Elijah himself would always have known the truth.

Others like to explain away miracles as physically rational, but with a spiritual message. The parents of a friend withdrew her from religious instruction lessons because the teacher explained the miracle of the feeding of the 5,000[127] as a kind of bring and share picnic; in this case the miracle was supposed to be in the sharing.

I think we are asking all the wrong questions here. Do you suppose that if I or Sister Macrina had possessed a camcorder it would have captured those angels? Certainly it took Ransom a fair time before he could see the *eldila* in Lewis' sci-fi fantasy. We are concerned with a different way of looking, similar in some ways to the manner in which an artist looks at reality, and so conveys, in for example a portrait, not just the physical features of the subject but the character as well. What is important is this: Are we willing to open our eyes and see in a new way and so engage with the mystery who is God?

SOME atheists want to remove the mystery from life, they want to view life through a microscope or a telescope or a magnetic resonance image.

Drawing conclusions from their prosaic view they can make staggering assertions about the nature of creation and life. For example:

> "Natural selection not only explains the *whole of life*; it also raises our consciousness to the power of science to explain how organised complexity can emerge from simple beginnings without any guidance."[128]

"Natural selection ... explains the whole of life"! Really?

As I write the postman knocks - once only – and delivers a package labelled "Please do not bend." I like our postman, it's an act of generosity to respect such requests. The package is from our friend Charles on Death Row. In it is a bundle of material: letters, *bons mots*, cartoons featuring Charles' alter-ego, "Charlie", and an enormous card, hence the "Please do not bend". Remember that Charles, for most of his life, has been a dangerous and violent man, a mercenary, murderer and more. The card has been bought from the prison canteen. It is 11 ¾ inches (30 cm) high, it is embossed and bears the words, "Just for you." Inside the card the work is all Charles'. There is a colour image of Charlie wearing his trademark "I ♥ Jesus" T-shirt, and, in monochrome, a few images and lines of prose:

> "When Charlie first came into your lives, he was telling people the right way of being a Christian but, without any of the qualities of being Christ like. But God knows Charlies heart and knew what He needed to make Charlie the true God fearing, God forgiven, hope filled, faithful, understanding Christian with a bounty of love, even for those that have wronged him ... So if God now calls Charlies author and artist home and you feel like crying, cry in joy, because Charlie through Charles has by Gods love ...become a true child of God full of love, compassion, forgiveness, true calm in every storm and real peace in his heart."[129]

These lines, like every aspect of our friendship with this remarkable man, raise some pertinent questions. How would someone who thinks natural selection explains all of life answer these?

- Does natural selection explain why Charles had to endure daily beatings and sexual humiliation from his mother until he ran away from home to fend for himself at the age of 14?
- Does natural selection explain how a woman could stand by and allow a man with whom she has just made love go to gaol for the rest of his life for a crime she knows he didn't commit?
- Does natural selection explain how a desperate and violent man, living in a world populated with other equally violent men, in conditions of appalling deprivation and with only the prospect of death before him, by lethal injection or natural causes, be so profoundly transformed?

I am not a scientist and I am happy to accept, if scientists say so, that physical life develops through natural selection. But I cannot accept that scientists, as scientists, can explain aspects of life such as the transformation of Charles. Atheists have a strange ally here. "Religious" America doesn't really believe in transformation either, otherwise they would not throw men like Charles on the scrap heap, even though they must be punished and society protected.

Some American Christians, religious people, prefer to take the mystery out of faith by making the Bible a scientific book. They want to know, in detail, all the answers. There are theme parks in Florida and Kentucky, for example, "recreating" the early chapters of Genesis:

> "Patrons walk through a lush re-creation of the Garden of Eden and see life-sized models of Adam and Eve frolic and get banished. Then it's on to the Great Flood, where animatronic workers are busy building Noah's giant ark..."[130]

The creationism industry is coming to the UK:

"A businesswoman has launched a £144 million mission to win youthful converts to Christianity by creating Britain's first biblical theme park. The complex would offer visitors the chance to slide down the Tower of Babel before climbing aboard Noah's Ark, parting the Red Sea and felling Goliath with a laser-guided slingshot… Children would also [experience] being swallowed by a whale …"[131]

The real mystery is how David got hold of that laser-guided sling!

There is an unholy alliance between atheist scientists and conservative Christians, strange bedfellows. Though they fight like cats about how they do it, they both want to take the mystery out of life; and neither can explain how, or even why, Charles has been transformed. That is a great mystery. Though most humanists oppose the death penalty and many conservative Christians, both Catholic and Evangelical, support it;[132] I suspect that both are indifferent to the fate of this human being and unmoved not only by the obvious transformation but by his naked humanity, it doesn't fit either of the moulds, scientific or religious. Charles' transformation is perhaps not as well-known as the transformation of Karla Faye Tucker, who had the advantage of being a woman.[133] Tucker was guilty of a horrible double murder, but experienced a genuine and life-changing conversion in prison which was evident to all who knew and met her. When she was executed no woman had been executed in Texas for over a hundred years. The (conservative Christian) governor of Texas (one George W Bush) refused to consider an appeal for clemency and even mocked her appeal.[134]

You could only mock someone is such a desperate situation if you don't understand the mystery of human life. Which, I would ask, is the more human here, Bush or Tucker? And isn't the transformation of both Charles and Karla Faye a miracle? The story is told of an interview with a converted alcoholic. The interviewer asked him,

"Do you believe that Jesus turned water into wine?"

"Water into wine I'm not sure about. But I do know this: He can turn beer into food and furniture." Is this human transformation not a miracle?

We can approach mystery through miracles and paradox but first we must engage with this: Can a Darwinian atheist explain the essence of humanity? Consider Kevin and Ken.

———•◦•———

KEVIN knows everyone, or so it seems to his friend Graham. When they visit the *Queen's Head* Kevin knows the name of the barman as well as the names of all the barmaids. He knows the drinkers at the bar by name and he knows which football team each supports and the relevant team's current standing in the table. He knows the names of the ticket clerk at the station and the checkout girls at the supermarket and whether they are married, and if they have children.

Kevin belongs to St Agatha's, the local church, too. He knows the names of all the members, which is more than the Vicar does. He can chat to the flower ladies about which blooms are in season and to the organist about today's anthem. He knows who has a sick relative and when members of the youth club are sitting GCSEs. Everyone likes Kevin.

The Vicar, Ken, on the other hand, is less popular. He doesn't visit as much as people think he should, he doesn't always answer his phone; and he has the embarrassing habit of asking, "How is it between you and God today?" when he meets people in the street.

Among the church members is Marjorie, who is an "expert" on the Royal Family, and Vicki, who knows "everything there is to know" about Cliff Richard, and old Fred, who can't remember anyone's name, or much about them. Then there's Dawn, whom no one, except possibly Kevin, knows, who keeps in the background and says little, though she's always there. Lastly there's Cameron, a psychotherapist who has several clients from within St Agatha's.

Knowing names is a wonderful gift to possess and not as mysterious as it seems, it can be learnt. A person's name is a precious possession; we like it when people remember our names; but some societies think that knowing a person's name gives you a certain power over them. If you don't believe this notice how often politicians on the *Today* programme use the interviewer's first name, whereas the interviewer must address the politician, at least on air, as Mr Smith or Mrs Jones.

The question is: Does knowing someone's name mean you know them? Does Marjorie, for example, know the Queen, or does Vicki know Cliff? And who knows the members of St Agatha's better: Kevin or Ken, or even Dawn or Cameron?

Names are important. When I was at theological college I knew a priest who was notorious for forgetting them. I rang him up to arrange next Sunday's preachment.

"What's your name? He asked.

"Richard."

We went on to discuss the arrangements for Sunday, after which he signed off: "Well, good to talk to you, Roger."

I didn't feel good that the priest had forgotten my name during the course of one short phone call. Names are important. But when I met the same priest six years later though he still didn't remember my name, he remembered *me* and that was worth a lot.

Does knowing someone's name indicate that we know them? At St Agatha's Marjorie knows all the names and titles of the Queen, she knows by what name various members of the Royal Family address her, she knows the names of all the corgis too. Vicki knows that Cliff used to be called Harry Webb and she also knows that no one ever calls him Harry unless they don't know him; Sir Cliff hates being called Harry. In the "blokish" culture of some pubs or workplaces almost everyone has an alias by which they are known, sometimes they have several aliases, one chap may be Bonzer in the pub, Mr Jones at the school where he teaches, Muggles to his wife and Sebastian to his mother.

So, who does know the members of St Agatha's better? That depends on how we continue our story. But we would never claim to really know someone unless we don't. Hold on to the paradox for later.

Kevin meets someone in the *Queen's Head* and he thinks he knows them because he knows their name, where they work and which football team they support. Ken has forgotten the names of a few members of St Agatha's, but he never presumes to say he knows them, he knows that the essence of a person is shrouded in mystery. Ken has been happily married for 37 years to Mary, but the longer he's married the less able he feels to describe her. She seems to grow more mysterious, not less.

> Those who know her, know her less
> The nearer her they get,[135]

There is, at the heart of every human being, a mysterious centre known only to God and, if the person is very spiritually aware, to themselves.

> "O LORD, you have searched me and you know me."[136]
> "Before I formed you in the womb I knew you."[137]
> "'How do you know me?' Nathanael asked.
> "Jesus answered. 'I saw you under the fig-tree before Philip called you.'
> "Then Nathanael declared, 'Rabbi, you are the Son of God.'"[138]

We approach mystery then through the mystery of humanity. It is an everyday phenomenon, we meet mystery when we mingle with fellow commuters on the train, when we get to work, when we put our children to bed and when we go to the *Queen's Head*. Kevin, who claims to know a lot of people, doesn't recognise the mystery as much as Ken; Cameron is not mystified but Dawn is awe-struck.

IF human beings are mysterious, how much more God? If God is God, then He is mystery, such profound mystery that we may as well stop writing and reading right away. Except, perhaps, for one thing. We have established that we can get a grasp of mystery by some understanding of the mystery of a human being. Suppose, then, that God (who is total mystery) decided to reveal Himself in a human being, in Jesus in fact.[139]

The Incarnation, that is God taking human form, reveals God. But it reveals God as a mystery. In the Incarnation Jesus the Son of God became human, fully human, not just smoke and mirrors. For the time being we may forget the cynical gibe, "the fatherless man". The Athanasian Creed, usually so impenetrable, puts it like this:

> "For the right faith is, that we believe and confess; that our Lord Jesus Christ, the Son of God, is God and Man;
> "God, of the Substance of the Father, begotten before the worlds: and Man, of the Substance of his Mother, born in the world;
> "Perfect God, and perfect Man …
> "Who although he be God and Man: yet he is not two, but one Christ."[140]

In fact it is not just the Creeds which make this paradoxical assertion, but Scripture too. Hebrews says, "The Son is... the exact representation of his [God's] being."[141] And goes on, "he had to be made like his brothers in every way."[142] Perfect Man and Perfect God. How can this be? If Jesus was human His knowledge was limited, He was subject to the same limitations and restrictions of any human being; He experienced life exactly as we experience it, all the joy and all the sorrow, all the pleasure and all the pain, all the love and all the hatred and rejection, all the success and all the failure, all the life and all the death that you and I experience. But if He was God then He must have been able to transcend human experience, to know everything, to be immune from suffering and temptation, and to be able to do anything He chose as well as to be exempt from death. Which is it? God or Man?

Christian theology says: Both. It's a paradox. Neither scientific nor religious people like paradox, on the religious side the Athanasian Creed tries hard to describe it, with limited success; religious Christians, liking paradox no more than the next person, try to resolve it. Some go heavy on the God bit, while others major on the Man side. Those who prefer Jesus as God cannot comprehend the cross so they describe it as illusion, Jesus only appeared to be suffering on the cross. They are called *Docetists* from the Greek *dokein,* "to seem". Those who major on the Man side have trouble thinking of Jesus as divine, this is a particular difficulty for fundamentalist cults like the Jehovah's Witnesses. Religious people like to have it all sewn up, but that won't do. You have to hold the paradox in tension or do violence to the person of Jesus. Holding a paradox in tension does not mean some limp compromise; it involves holding fast to the extremes, all of them. This is the dynamic *via media* on which Anglicanism is supposed to be based, though in reality it too often comes over as the bland compromise.

In fact people of faith will be no strangers to the mystery of paradox. Here are some more: God is transcendant, in other words beyond our understanding; and God is immanent, here with us in spirit (Spirit?). The Bible says both: God said to Moses, "no-one may see me and live."[143] But a few verses earlier we can read, "The LORD would speak to Moses face to face, as a man speaks with his friend."[144] The critical theologian may assume that in editing the text the redactor has uncritically placed contradictory passages in proximity to each other. Those who understand mystery know that this nameless editor knew exactly what he was doing.

Once again religious people like to resolve the paradox. You can see it in the form of worship. In some churches, usually those we call "Catholic" or "Orthodox", God is awesome, transcendent, distant. This is expressed by placing the altar behind a screen and obscuring the celebration of the Sacrament by positioning the priest with his (it usually is "his") back to the people, and by expressing worship in genuflections and other signs of submission and respect. No one may see God's face and live. In other churches, usually "Evangelical" or "Charismatic" churches, the worship is chummy and informal, God is a mate who speaks to us as to a friend. Since God is neither one nor the other, but both, both in the extreme, we see these varying approaches as religious denominationalism, and not the true expression of the mystery of faith.

While we are thinking of paradox, here's the big one. As much blood as ink has been spilled over this: God is Three and God is One, the Trinity. How can God be both Three and One? It's a paradox and you'll have to do better than look at a clover leaf, or imagine H_2O as ice, water and steam to explain it. Since religious people don't like paradox, they resolve it and, once again, we get denominationalism. The theology of the Trinity is for religious people; people of faith accept mysterious paradox as the way in which we experience God.

Living with paradox and trying to hold it in tension is one way we can experience the mystery of God, who is so far above our understanding that we can never comprehend Him; if we could, God would be on our level, the same as you and I. I can't speak for you, but I know I would make a very bad god indeed.

———•—•—•———

SO much for paradox, but we can't leave mystery without grappling with what Christians in the eastern tradition call "The Mysteries". The word Sacrament is derived from Latin and is used, therefore, only in the western church; eastern Christians call sacraments "mysteries". They have a much more open approach too, not for them merely seven sacraments, far less only two.[145]

The term "hocus-pocus" is a corruption of the words of consecration from the Latin Mass (*Hoc est corpus meus* – this is my body). That alone should alert us to the weight of superstition that used to attach to the sacraments, and perhaps still does. In response to superstition the reformers, Cranmer among them, tried to demystify the sacraments.

> to auoyde the prophanacion and dysordre … it is not ment
> therby, that any adoracion is done, or oughte to bee done…

> they [the bread and wine] remayne styll in theyr naturall subs-
> taunces, and therefore may not be adored[146]

Demystification has been taken even further today in the intensely casual administration found in some evangelical churches. We may well remember that evangelical radicals from the past had the greatest respect for the sacraments, among them, Cranmer himself, and John Wesley who recommended taking Communion several times a week. It was not the mystery they sought to destroy but the superstition. The mystery remains.

There is a debate, in the Church of England today, about the admission of children to Holy Communion before Confirmation. Some people think that young people should not be allowed to receive until they understand what they are doing. I would say, though, that no one should be admitted until they know they *don't* understand. Which of us can honestly say we fully comprehend what is going on in the sacraments? We know the potted definition from the Catechism, "an outward and visible sign of an inner and spiritual grace." But what does it mean? Talking of sexuality and love John Sanford said, "I know a lot about sex. I know a lot about love. I know a lot about transference and when I add them together, I know nothing at all."[147] He could have been talking about the sacraments. We may know a lot about liturgy, a lot about theology, a lot about philosophy, a lot about church history and putting them together still know nothing.

Eucharist is the central sacrament. Whether we call it *Mass* or *Holy Communion* or the *Lord's Supper* or the *Breaking of Bread*, it's all the same. In the Eucharist the ordinary things of life, bread and wine, become extraordinary. The same applies to the water of Baptism or the oil of anointing. *How* this happens is a mystery. And, just as we will never describe a sound or a colour (see chapter 3) we will never describe a sacrament. Take transubstantiation for example, does this describe what happens? How many understand it? In fact it is supposed to be something like this: In the Eucharist the elements (bread and wine) are made up of *form* and *substance*. The form is what is perceived through the senses, the substance is the inner meaning. In Sacramental theology the form remains the same, in other words bread is still bread, it feels like bread, tastes like bread and so on; but the substance has changed, the inner meaning has altered so that the bread becomes, in substance, the Body of Christ. This is denied in the Book of Common Prayer 1552 (retained in 1662), but not 1549:

> The Sacramentall bread and wyne, they reamyne still in theyr verye naturall subsauces ...

In actual fact it's not just Roman Catholics who believe that something changes, whether you call it "substance" or something else. Years ago I heard Eric Delve talk about his experience as a child in the Brethren. Every time they "broke bread" the elder explained that "nothing happened" and this was simply a memorial in obedience to the command of Jesus, "Do this is remembrance of me."[148] One day Eric wandered in from Sunday School a little early and found the leftover bread lying in the vestry. Being hungry he started to eat; after all, he reasoned, this was only ordinary bread. Unfortunately an elder discovered him eating and cried out, "You can't eat that, that's special." So it turns out that even Brethren believe in transubstantiation after all. So what? Isn't it enough to know that we all perceive something mysterious in the sacraments? Isn't it enough to know that Presbyterians celebrate the Eucharist only four times a year as a mark of how special it is, while Roman Catholics celebrate it every day for the same reason?

In some churches they use special tiny wafers for bread and wine "specially fermented for the altar". In some they drink from a common cup and in others they each have a little individual glasses, in yet others the laity cannot be trusted with wine at all. People can fall out over such things. It is as if we do everything we can to rob this symbol of its power. The symbolic point of a sacrament is that *ordinary* things become extraordinary. The Book of Common Prayer decrees that "the Bread be such as is usual to be eaten".[149] Because the most basic ingredients are used in sacraments, at least they were basic in the Mediterranean culture of the 1st Century, bread, wine, water, olive oil, the mystical element is all the more up to God. We do not need water from the river Jordan to be Baptised, and we do not need special, if foul-tasting, wine for Communion, we need eyes to see, ears to hear and a heart to understand that in these wonder events God is present.

Neither are these mysteries merely seven. Sacraments, mysteries, are all around us. For a Pentecostal, speaking in tongues is a sacrament, though they wouldn't use the word. The point is made by Simon Tugwell. His essay[150] concludes:

> Sacraments are meant to be human acts, in which human words are spoken; but they should also be a means by which we are brought to realise that human acts are only fully human in so far as they get beyond mere self-assertiveness, and find their roots in the act of God himself; and that human words only carry weight… in so far as they proceed from the Word of God which itself proceeds eternally from the Silence of the Father.

Morton and Barbara Kelsey conclude that sex is, or is meant to be, a sacrament, the union of lovers enabling them to experience a sign of union with God.[151]

We could say that the experience of angels in a tree is also sacramental, the tree being the "outward and visible sign". Indeed we will go further; wherever there is mystery there is sacrament. Mystery itself is the sign that God is.

In the next chapter we look at the paradox of discipline, which (paradoxically) is, or should be, the antithesis of religion. It is a necessary interjection to the flow of our argument, which will resume in earnest in chapter 9 when we pick up with Faith as Relationship.

Endnotes

[118] *Eternal Echoes* John O'Donohue (Bantam 1998 p 52)
[119] *A Tree Full of Angels* Macrina Wiederkehr (Harper and Row 1988 p 83)
[120] *Out of the Silent Planet* CS Lewis (Pan 1963 edition p 88)

[121] *Ibid* p 137

[122] The work of the Alistair Hardy Institute among others.

[123] *God of Surprises* Gerard W Hughes (DLT 1985 p 3)

[124] I have altered several elements in the interests of anonymity.

[125] *Miracles* CS Lewis (Fontana 1960 pp 7f)

[126] 1 Kings 18:16ff

[127] Matthew 14:13-21, Mark 6:30-44, Luke 9:10-17, John 6:1-13 This is the only miracle (apart from the Resurrection) included in all four Gospels.

[128] *The God Delusion* Richard Dawkins (Bantam 2006 p 116 my italics)

[129] I have kept the original spelling and punctuation

[130] www.secularism.org.uk/82272.html

[131] *The Times* 28th March 2005

[132] For a rare intelligent justification see, for example, *God's Punishment and Ours: The Morality of Judicial Participation in the Death Penalty* Antonin Scalia in *Religion and the Death Penalty* ed Erik Owens, John Carlson and Eric Elshtain (Eerdmans 2004). Most apologia are far less rational.

[133] *The Death of Innocents* Sister Helen Prejean (Canterbury Press 2006 pp 244-250)

[134] In an interview with journalist Tucker Carlson, Bush gave this account of Karla Faye Tucker's TV interview with Larry King. King asked,

"'What would you say to Governor Bush?'

"'What did Tucker answer?' Carlson asked.

"'Please,' Bush whimpered, his lips pursed in mock desperation, 'please don't kill me.'"

(Quoted in Prejean *Ibid*)

[135] Emily Dickenson *Poems 1400* quoted in *New Heaven? New Earth?* Simon Tugwell et al (DLT 1976 p 121)

[136] Psalm 139:1

[137] Jeremiah 1:5

[138] John 1:48f

[139] Hebrews 1:1-4

[140] *Quicunque Vult* Book of Common Prayer

[141] Hebrews 1:3

[142] Hebrews 2:17

[143] Exodus 33:23

[144] Exodus 33:11

[145] Roman Catholics and Anglicans of a catholic persuasion recognise as sacraments: Eucharist, Baptism, Confirmation, Ordination, Marriage, Anointing and Reconciliation (Confession). Protestants with equal rigidity recognise only the first two, the so-called "Dominical" sacraments which appear in the Gospels.

[146] Rubric in the Book of Common Prayer 1552, retained in 1662. This rubric is absent in the BCP 1549, although there is a rubric concerning superstition.

[147] Quoted in *Sacrament of Sexuality* Morton and Barbara Kelsey (Element 1991 p 1)

[148] 1 Corinthians 11:24. This is the earliest account of the Lord's Supper, earlier than the Gospel accounts.

[149] Book of Common Prayer, rubrics for Holy Communion

[150] *The Speech-giving Spirit* Simon Tugwell in *New Heaven? New Earth?* (DLT 1976 pp 154f)

[151] *Sacrament of Sexuality* Morton Kelsey and Barbara Kelsey (Element 1986)

Chapter 8
FAITH AS DISCIPLINE

I AM standing at the top of a flight of stairs. Behind me an open door admits some light, but the stairs descend into utter darkness. I imagine I hear a voice calling, "Come." I dither and grab the handrail; I do not like darkness. A gust of wind catches the door and it slams shut. Then I remember that there is no handle on the inside. Now the darkness is absolute; I cannot see my fingers, even an inch from my eyes. I imagine the voice is calling again, "Come." Clasping the rail even tighter I begin the descent, one slow and halting step at a time.

After a very long descent I arrive at the bottom of the stairs. I feel around me, there seem to be no walls, nor ceiling, only a brick floor. Now I realise that I have lost my bearings and can no longer find my way back to the stairs. I cannot retrace my steps in the utter blackness.

Then I hear the voice again, or I imagine I do, "Come." And I think I see the tiniest pin-prick of light, almost too small to pick out, here one moment, gone the next. I stumble towards the light, one hesitant step after another...

I could put it like this:

Night

I push the door and walk
    Hesitantly.
I hold the door and baulk
    Timidly.
A gust, eery dark gales
    And slams.
Darkness, I grope the blackness.

> Now there is no door, no return
> >   Only darkness, silence
> No echo, no touch, no sense.
> >   Blackness. Nothing.
> Emptiness.
>
> And as I look the merest
> >   Glimmer rises far away ...

MOST people have never experienced absolute darkness. There is always some light - of stars or the glimmer from a curtained window, perhaps. I have experienced total darkness down a coal mine. There are almost no deep mines left in Britain today, but I was lucky enough to go down one before they closed. It's an unnerving experience, in our case the coalface was not only deep but also several miles from the shaft, we made the journey by train, it took half-an-hour. I have also been down a museum pit where miners scratch a living by showing visitors round a small portion of a once great mine. Underground, when the lights go out it is dark. Our guide in the museum told us how early miners would hack out the coal, using only the spark from a flint for light.

St John of the Cross used the symbol of darkness, or better "Night", to describe part of the journey of the soul to God. Night is not a time of consolation, nevertheless John welcomed it as a friend because he could see it as the way to God.

> "Dark of the night, my guise,
> fairer by far than dawn when stars grow dim!
> Night that has unified
> The Lover and the Bride,
> Transforming the beloved into him.[152]

John did indeed suffer, mainly at the hands of his Carmelite brothers who for several months imprisoned and beat him and sought to undermine his faith, until he managed to escape. But this is a metaphor, in reality "Night" is a spiritual experience, a "purifying passage that an individual undergoes which transforms one kind of life into another."[153] Rolheiser, in a helpful essay,[154] compares this stage of spiritual growth to the period in a human love relationship when the sense of being "in love" ends and a couple are left wondering what is next in their relationship. At this point some couples give up and each looks for someone else with whom to fall in love, others stick it out and eventually grow into a deeper love. For some the desolation of night endures for years. John's friend, Teresa of Avila, endured twelve years in the spiritual desert, following a serious illness. I experienced twelve years in the wilderness once, but when I re-read my journal I found it had started a week last Friday! If a couple of weeks of desolation feel like twelve years, I can't even imagine what twelve years must feel like.

In chapter 5 I suggested that faith is like adventures, those "nasty, disturbing, uncomfortable things…". In adventures there almost always comes a time when all the joy seems to have gone out of it, when the enterprise seems sheer grind and we lose sight of the goal. When in 1999 I was cycling alone from Totnes to Santander, the first couple of days, crossing Brittany, offered more or less unrelenting rain. When you are cycle-camping rain eventually gets everywhere, there is no refuge. My tent was wet, my clothes were wet, my towel was sodden, my sleeping bag was damp, even my maps and my Bible were limp. After three days I could hardly see the point of the journey at all, it seemed like pig-headed folly, a waste of a perfectly good holiday. Luckily I kept going because, as the guide book had suggested it might, after crossing the Loire the weather turned fair, almost for the rest of the journey. Getting wet is hardly great suffering, especially when you know you could always check into a hotel; this is the difference between my holiday and a real adventure. In the real thing there is no hotel to check into. Many proper adventurers suffer life-threatening trials yet manage to keep going to the end. Spiritual adventures are just as real and the difficulties are just as hard to overcome. Perseverance demands as much in the spiritual as in the physical realm.

HOW is it possible to keep going when testing comes? is my question. This is where that troubling little word discipline comes in. When you read the word "discipline" you may be thinking: "Ah, yes! I knew a priest could not keep away from religion for very long." But what I am talking about is very different from religion though you'll have to keep reading to find out how.

If you thought that discipline is like religion you'd be wrong. Discipline is being a *disciple*, in this case a disciple, a follower, of Jesus Christ. The words discipline and disciple, as you can see, are closely linked. Forget all those images which come into your mind along with the word discipline; forget the humiliating corporal punishment of your school days (if you're as old as me, that is); forget the unquestioning obedience of the soldier; forget the joyless religiosity found in some churches, all of which are sometimes mistaken for discipline. Discipline is following Jesus Christ and recognising the desire to follow Him as the *deepest* desire. People of faith, as opposed to people of religion, are in touch with the deep-down desire for God who made us in His image and implanted within us the desire for union with Him. We progress on the journey through being a disciple, a follower, and that involves discipline which itself involves desire. Many disciples have suffered unmentionable physical hardships and persecutions. We, none of us, know how we would respond in such a situation. That's the sort of thing you only find out when you get to it. For most of us the temptations are far less obvious but, consequently, more insidious. When you know that to be a disciple of Jesus is to risk imprisonment, torture or death you at least know where you stand. When, on the other hand, the worst you face is indifference (the spiritual equivalent of a good wetting when you're cycle-camping), you are not faced with the same stark choice and that makes it harder not to wimp out. Even more insidious are the little voices which try to draw us away from our original intention to pray or worship.

Discipline is how we keep going joyfully, whether facing persecution or the lures of comfort and ease; discipline is how we separate out the deepest desire from the nagging and insistent desires, for example, for a new car, a new dress, yet another bar of chocolate or a luxury holiday. These are not bad things in themselves, but the disciple knows that real satisfaction can only come from following Jesus. Discipline, to use Rolheiser's analogy, is how a husband, experiencing the dryness which comes when the feeling of being "in love" is spent, knows that he desires union with his wife more than he desires a fling with that dishy secretary.

------•-•-•------

AFTER a *Closer to God* course one of the participants was unimpressed. "I don't need all this fancy stuff," he complained, "I don't need to set aside time to pray; I just natter to God through the day." Nattering to God through the day is fine. But beware, it takes little to turn our attention elsewhere, as the demon Screwtape observed to Wormwood, his apprentice, "You no longer need a good book ... to keep him from his prayers... a column of advertisements in yesterday's paper will do."[155] Then imagine, instead of talking about God, this man was talking about his wife. "I don't need to spend quality time with her, I just chat away to her while I get on with the day." I hardly need to mention that we are describing here a marriage in trouble, or in danger of trouble. When a man is in love with a woman, or even after he has grown past the "in love" stage, he desires to sit down and talk to her. So, a man or woman in love with God will want to spend time with Him, the best time. Discipline is being in touch with this desire and acting on it. As Screwtape reminds us, it takes little to divert desire. I know I really want to pray, but I also want to solve the Sudoku puzzle in the paper...

------•-•-•------

THE first and most important quality of discipleship is that it involves the whole of life. God intends us to be alive and true life is only possible in conjunction with integrity, wholeness, holiness. The disciple sees no distinction between what happens in prayer, in worship and in life in general. I remember few sermons, not even my own. People sometimes say to me, "You remember when you said ...?" And I truthfully reply, "No, I don't, remind me." Even then I'm not entirely sure it is accurate, or even authentic. However I can remember a sermon I heard in 1976 in the Anglican church in Tehran. The preacher was the Bishop of Iran,

Hassan Deqani-Tafti. I can't, of course, remember the exact words, but I remember clearly how he told us about his abortive attempts to pray while at theological college. He even, apparently, set aside an hour a day for prayer. So far so good, but the future Bishop discovered that his prayers were invariably dry. Bishop Hassan told us how he had discovered the reason for the dryness; he had been regarding the other 23 hours of the day as his own. No wonder he didn't grow in prayer; the disciple is a disciple 24 hours a day or not at all. That means that there is complete integration between what happens in church and what happens afterwards, Sunday and Monday are all of a piece. The hour or so in church on Sunday, even if you go every week, is not your "duty" for the week, conveniently forgotten when you arrive in the office next day; duty is religion. The hour or so in church focuses the whole week; it hallows the time; it is symbolic that the whole of life belongs to God. In the same way, the daily time of prayer is symbolic that the whole day is God's. In the context of the hour, or whatever, of quality prayer, nattering away to God through the day then takes on a completely different significance.

> Take my life, and let it be
> Consecrated, Lord, to thee.
> Take my moments and my days;
> Let them flow in *ceaseless* praise.
>
> Take my silver and my gold;
> Not a mite would I withhold.[156]

I don't imagine Frances Havergal was familiar with the *Spiritual Exercises* of St Ignatius Loyola, but in them we find something similar:

> "Take, Lord, and receive all my liberty, my memory, my understanding, and my entire will, all that I have and possess. Thou hast given all to me. To Thee, O Lord, I return it. All is Thine, dispose of it wholly according to Thy will. Give me Thy love and Thy grace, for this is sufficient for me."[157]

David L Fleming SJ, in his translation, has "… all that I have and call my own…"[158]

This prayer is placed at the end of the fourth "week" of the Exercises, pretty much the last thought after thirty days of concentrated time with God. It is the goal of the disciple to be wholly given to God, in all of our being, thoughts, possessions, desires.

That involves everything. The big mistake of the religious person is to think that it means being pious or churchy. In fact discipleship means setting aside time to pray daily, setting aside time to worship with the community of believers weekly, then it means getting out and living to the full. This is ceaseless praise. But be careful that you really want what you think you want. There are countless myths which warn us about what to wish for, we might get it and, here's the rub, we might not like it. The myth of King Midas, for example, tells us that he wished everything he touched would turn to gold and, too late, discovered that gold is not the best material for most of our needs.

Here's a real example. When I was in the Hallé Orchestra we were offered the chance to play at the reopening of the Palace Theatre in Manchester. It was very tempting, there would be two three-hour rehearsals and, the same evening, a performance in front of Prince Charles. Kiri te Kanawa was on the bill along with a host of other stars. The show would be televised, and all that meant that a huge fee was on offer, equivalent, I seem to remember, to two weeks wages for a day's work. The trouble was, it was a Sunday, and though we often worked on Sunday evenings, on this occasion the first rehearsal would be at 10.00 am. I dithered and decided that, since I was a person of faith not religion, I would accept the offer. I even (religiously) went to the 8.00 Holy Communion first. I have always regretted my decision and whenever I pass the Palace Theatre remember it. I know, that as a child of grace not of Law, I do not *have* to go to church; but what I suppressed was my *desire* to go to church. I ended up choosing money and the presence of celebrity which was certainly not my deepest desire. In the event it wasn't fun, the rehearsals overran (more money but also more work) and we had to stay on afterwards to re-record for TV those parts of the show which had gone wrong. It was a very long day and I don't think I enjoyed the extra money.

On that day I made use of my freedom and it brought me unhappiness. That doesn't mean I have to be frightfully religious to prevent these things happening again. Before I met Jesus I used to think that I couldn't be a Christian because I would have to give up all the things I enjoyed. I have since discovered that I did have to give some things up, but they turned out to be the things I didn't really enjoy at all. So much of the unredeemed life is doing things we don't enjoy to impress people we don't like; or buying stuff we don't like because it has an acceptable logo. It is the most underhand trick of the advertising industry to lure us to spend money on what does not satisfy.

> "Come, all you who are thirsty,
>   come to the waters;
> and you who have no money,
>   come, buy and eat!
> Come, buy wine and milk
>   Without money and without cost.
> Why spend money on what is not bread,
>   And your labour on what does not satisfy?"[159]

Discipline is making those choices which are in harmony with our deepest desires and so bring us peace and joy, if not always ease and comfort.

————•◦•————

I HAVE noticed that there are two qualities invariably present in real disciples: They always have a great sense of humour; not the nasty sneering "humour" which laughs *at* others, but the easy humour which laughs *with* others and *at* one's own absurdities. Secondly they always have a zest for life. Real disciples *enjoy* life, all of life, and make choices which enhance it. When they go to the theatre they are not thinking, "What would Jesus do?" they are too absorbed in the play. My father used to say of a rather pious colleague, "He probably prays before he makes love." That may well have been so but when a real disciple makes love he is not thinking about God he is thinking about his lover.

"Ceaseless praise" is not the state of constant formal prayer, or piety. I once went to my spiritual director in a state of some anxiety. I was worn out from overwork and depressed. He wisely commented, "When you get up 'there' He's not going to ask you how many parishioners you visited, He's going to say, 'How did you enjoy my creation?'" There is a humility in the disciple, not the mock humility of Uriah Heap, but the easy humility which recognises that it is not our own effort (ie religion) which ushers in the Kingdom of God, but the grace of God with which the disciple co-operates, that is faith. When I engage in a surfeit of religious activities, or "ministry" I am indulging myself in religion. CS Lewis comments, "She's the sort of woman who lives for others – you can tell the others by their hunted expression."[160] The disciple lives a life of balance in which work, play, sleep and recreation all have a place, in which concern for the self is in balance with concern for others. This is the aim of the Rule of St Benedict.[161] To post-modern eyes Benedict's Rule may appear overly religious, but the ideal, written down in the 6th Century, is strangely attractive today, as the recent TV series *The Monastery* showed. Benedict attempted to produce a rule which would put all of life in balance. There is provision for leisure as well as work as well as prayer. Our college chapel carried on the lintel the Benedictine motto. As we went in we read: *Orare est laborare* – to pray is to work. After the service we read: *Laborare est orare*. Benedict could have included in this formula leisure, sleep, eating and more. Over a thousand years later George Herbert wrote:

> "Teach me, my God and King,
>   In all things thee to see,
> And what I do in anything,
>   To do it as for thee."[162]

To do things "as for thee" does not mean being frightfully pious, it involves integrity. The Christian gardener, for example, is a good gardener; being a good gardener, being a good steward of the earth, is in itself holy.[163]

WE have established that being a disciple is a 24/7 occupation which involves living life in every aspect well. But we cannot ignore the fact that discipleship involves a certain disciplined regularity. The life of prayer will not just happen, no matter how hard we natter. If we want to grow in prayer we will need to establish some sort of discipline. In chapter 5 I considered the importance of place and posture and stillness in prayer.

We need to establish a regularity because it is natural that our feelings will ebb and flow, Ignatius called these swings of mood consolation and desolation. Our feelings are not unimportant, on the contrary they are indicators which can put us in touch with our deepest desire. Ignatius discovered their importance while convalescing after painful surgery to repair his legs, which had been shattered during the siege of Pamplona. With hours to while away and little to divert his attention he took to indulging in lengthy daydreams. Sometimes he would dream of "what he was to do in the service of a certain lady... the witty love poems, the words he would say to her ..."[164] Other times he would dream of outdoing the saints in holiness, "St Francis did this, so I must do it; St Dominic did this, so must I do it."[165] After a while he noticed that the dreams of wooing great ladies were like Chinese dinners, very satisfying at the time, but it wasn't long before he wanted another one. The dreams of holiness, however, were like roast beef, satisfying at the time and for hours to come. He actually put it like this (he referred to himself in the third person):

> "There was this difference: that when he was thinking about that worldly stuff he would take much delight, but after he left it aside ... he would find himself dry and discontented. But when [thinking] about ... other rigours he was seeing the saints had done, not only used he to be consoled while in such thoughts, but he would remain content and happy even after having left them aside."[166]

From these observations of his own soul he concluded that his deepest desire was for holiness and so, in the sick-room of the family castle, a great and remarkable conversion followed. From his observations Igna-

tius eventually compiled "rules for the discernment of spirits" by which
we may be helped to use our feelings to identify our deepest desires
and, and thus the will of God.

Feelings, then, are important. But when we are ruled by our feelings
rather than our real desires we take for a spiritual director the devil
himself. Suppose we only pray when we "feel like it"; we will end up
praying little if at all. Discipline involves connecting with and obeying
our deeper desires even when other desires obscure them. Ignatius left
us plenty of practical advice about how we might achieve this. He tells
us we should not, when in desolation, change decisions made in time
of consolation; that we should pray *more* in time of desolation, not less;
we should, in other words, show "the evil spirit" who's boss.[167]

Whatever our feelings then, we should set aside a time for God *every*
day. It is best if this is the same time each day, the time when we are
most alert, not when we are falling asleep. For "morning people" that
means first thing, for "night owls" it means late in the evening. Some
people even find it best to pray in the afternoon. And make it the
same length of time each day, otherwise we will pray long when we
feel good and so indulge ourselves, and short when we are depressed.
This time can be gradually extended as our walk with God progresses
and we grow deeper into Him. We may, for example, start with a mere
ten minutes. Over time this can grow into twenty, thirty even sixty
minutes a day or more.

NOT long after my encounter with "Josh" on the train I began to sink
into a state of depression caused by a temporary lull in my career and a
reverse in love. I am now grateful for this dry time in particular, since I
got through it I knew in a way I might otherwise not have known, that
my desire for God was real. I once asked my spiritual director about
these dry patches. She replied, "God seems to withdraw the sense of
His presence in order to know whether we seek Him for Himself, or
for the pleasure it gives us." There have been times in my life when
prayer has been a continual delight. Then I look forward to my prayer

times and hardly want to stop when time is up. This is marvellous, but dangerous if not handled with care. It is easy then to sink into praying for the sheer pleasure of it, into self-indulgence in fact; I pray because it gives me a buzz, which is like the worst excesses of new-age self-fulfilment rhetoric, it is narcissistic and has little to do with God; so long as I feel good I could be worshipping the devil himself. God likes to give consolation, but He also brings times of desolation too, then we (and He) really find out if we seek God Himself, or an impostor, whether we are a disciple of Jesus Christ, following Him on the way to His Father, or whether we are disciples of someone or something else altogether.

FOR the use of those seeking to build a rhythmic and disciplined life I have compiled a check-list, which I call, with deliberate double meaning, "Rhythm Rules". It would be a huge mistake to use this check-list religiously; then it would lead to slavery. But, used prayerfully and faithfully it can be an aid to building the sort of "rule" which helps us live a life of faith. If you want to use this simple questionnaire, be sure to get really still before attempting to engage with the questions. Then be sure to answer prayerfully, and finally be sure to reflect on your answers in an attitude of prayer before making dramatic resolutions. Adrian Plass in his fictional *Sacred Diary* decided to pray for two hours after the rest of the family were in bed. Very soon he ended up falling asleep over "a long Albanian film with sub-titles, set in a kitchen."[168] The same fate awaits many who make impulsive commitments.

> "Suppose one of you wants to build a tower. Will he not first sit down and estimate the cost to see if he has enough money to complete it? For if he lays a foundation and is not able to finish it, everyone who sees it will ridicule him."[169]

For prayerful use ONLY then, here is *Rhythm Rules*

o   I consider the rhythm of my life. What percentage of my time is spent in the following ways? To make it easier, call 1 hour per day 4% (NB there may be some overlap – eg Family time could also be leisure time, and the figures may add up to more or less than 100):

Work:	%
Leisure:	%
Church activities:	%
Sleep:	%
Prayer:	%
Family:	%
Worship:	%
Study:	%

o   Is this a satisfactory allocation of time

o   If not, what is stopping me changing it?

o   Do I try to live on an endless high? Or do I accept the lows and highs?

o   How often do I have a rest day? How do I spend it?

o   Can I face pain and find in it opportunities for growth?

o   When I meet others do I do all the talking? Or all the listening?

o   When I pray do I allow time for God to speak?

o   Do I regularly reflect on my experience?

o   Is there a discernible relationship between my prayer and the ordinary events of daily life? How do they inter-relate?

o   Am I the same person with my friends, with my colleagues, with my family, in my church? Should I be?

o   How often do I laugh? Is it enough?

o   I imagine that tomorrow, as if by magic, I will be able to do absolutely anything I wish, without restraint. How will I spend the time?

o   When did I last do something I **really** wanted to do?

o   Are there any areas about which it might be worthwhile to seek the help of a prayer guide/director? If so, what are they?

Endnotes

[152] *Dark Night* St John of the Cross (translation Marjorie Flower OCD in *The Impact of God* Iain Matthew – Hodder and Stoughton 1995 p 53)

[153] Ronald Rolheiser *John and Human Development* in *A Fresh Approach to St John of the Cross* Ed John McGowan (St Pauls 1993 p 33)

[154] *Ibid*

[155] *The Screwtape Letters* CS Lewis (Bles 1942 p 63)

[156] *Take my Life* Frances Ridley Havergal. I note that in at least one hymn book verse 4, "Take my silver..." is asterisked as an optional verse!

[157] *The Spiritual Exercises* Ignatius Loyola (tr Louis J Puhl SJ Loyola University Press 1951 p 102)

[158] *Draw Me Into Your Friendship – The Spiritual Exercises a Literal Translation and a Contemporary Reading.* David L Fleming SJ (Institute of Jesuit Sources 1996 p 177)

[159] Isaiah 55:1f

[160] *The Screwtape Letters* CS Lewis (Bles 1942 p 135)

[161] *The Rule of St Benedict* Tr Abbot Parry OSB (Gracewing 1990)

[162] *The Elixir* George Herbert in *The Temple* (Classics of Western Spirituality SPCK 1981 p 311)

[163] Genesis 2:15

[164] *Autobiography* Ignatius Loyola in *Personal Writings* Tr Munitiz and Endean (Penguin 1996 pp 14f)

[165] *ibid* p 15

[166] *ibid* p 15

[167] See *The Spiritual Exercises* §§ 313-336

[168] *The Sacred Diary of Adrian Plass (Aged 37 ¾)* Adrian Plass (Marshall Pickering 1987 p 127)

[169] Luke 14:28f

Chapter 9
FAITH AS RELATIONSHIP

YOU have met many of my friends during the course of this book, not all of them by name. You have met, among others, Monica my wife, Martin my oldest friend and Charles my friend on Death Row; you have also met Pauline, Ian, Doreen, Chris, Veronica, Ted, Christina, Paul, Polly, Don and Lyn and several others - this is a very personal book, faith is personal.

One whom you have met several times is Charles. I met Charles through LifeLines, an organisation founded in 1987 by Jan Arriens after he saw, by chance, a documentary on BBC TV called *Fourteen Days in May*. This courageous film, directed by Paul Hamann, follows the last two weeks in the life of Edward Earl Johnson, a young black man executed by poison gas in the state of Mississippi. Johnson was innocent and Hamann went back to Mississippi the following year (1988) and uncovered the identity of the real murderer. Three other Death Row inmates appeared in *Fourteen Days in May* and Arriens was so moved by the film that he started writing to them. LifeLines now has more than 1,600 members and most of the 3,800 Death Row prisoners in the USA who want one have a British penfriend. Some of these correspondents, where state regulations allow it, cross the Atlantic to visit their penfriends. Monica and I have visited four times to date and found our visits enormously enriching. LifeLines is about relationships, particularly with those who are classed as less than human and fit only for death. Our friendships challenge the pervading notion that these violent criminals (though it is certain that a significant number on Death Row are innocent[170]) are fit only for hell, having committed, it is supposed, the unforgivable sin.

According to Dale Recinella the Death Penalty in the USA is derived from slavery;[171] it is, at the very least, a reflection of a deeply divided society and thus a denial of relationship. If, on a map of the USA, you were to colour in the States which use the Death Penalty the most, you would find that it almost mirrors the map of the Confederacy, in other words the States which, until the Civil War, allowed slavery. Thirty-eight States and the Federal Government have capital punishment on their statute books but, with the exception of California, those who use it systematically are all previously slaving States. This is not a book about Death Row, there are plenty of those already, but the facts remain that Death Rows across the USA are filled with the mentally retarded, psychologically ill, ethnic minorities (especially African Americans) and above all the poor. There are no rich people on Death Row. In other words these are the faceless poor.

The United States has been in the forefront of the "neocon" revolution. According to neocons, in life it's everyone for themselves; it is, therefore, wrong to spend tax dollars on health care, on any more than the most basic education, or on other public services except the police, prisons and the military. According to the theory society is at its most stable when everyone selfishly looks after their own interests. Thus co-operation is dangerous and any hint of it damned as "communism". Poverty is necessary to this philosophy, there are no winners without there being losers too. Poverty, though, is hidden away from the gaze of most Americans. One of the side-effects of Hurricane Katrina, which struck and devastated New Orleans, was that Americans saw, many of them for the first time, the poverty in their midst. 100,000 people in New Orleans did not possess a car, yet the evacuation plan made no provision for non-car owners who were left to drown or to be herded into the Superdrome like cattle.

But as we consider relationships we will have to consider not just the "you-me" relationships of friendship, marriage and the rest, but also the relationships of communities, and especially relationships with the unseen poor. The Gospel has a distinct bias towards the poor, and the poor have so much to teach us about community relationships. When you are poor you have to co-operate to survive.

I may seem to be anti-American in my remarks thus far. But the same issues surrounding the invisible poor are as relevant in the United

Kingdom as in the United States. Since Mrs (now Lady) Thatcher became Prime Minister in 1979 there has been a steady erosion of the sense of community and a corresponding growth in individualism. Mrs Thatcher's remark, in a popular women's magazine, that there is no such thing as society sums up the theory of the revolution. The Blair government, nominally Labour, continued the revolution Mrs Thatcher instigated and since 1997 the gap between rich and poor has grown to obscene proportions. This gives the message that some people are "worth" millions of times more than most others. When, for example, the CEO of Barclays helped himself to an annual salary in excess of £200M in 2006 it probably said to the tellers and clerks in Barclays that they are almost worthless.

But God says there is such a thing as society and that the Church, as a prophetic community, should model it.[172] The Thatcher revolution is profoundly opposed to the Biblical ideal in which every person has equal and infinite value in the eyes of God; to ignore, undervalue, or reject any person is a direct affront to God who is father to all, and especially the poor.[173]

Death Row, along with Guantanamo Bay, is home to the poorest of the world's poor. Here are people who have nothing; their food is inedible, they are caged like animals in a tiny coop without adequate heating or any air-conditioning, in some States these cages are underground so their occupants don't even see natural light. In addition prisoners have little of no access to health care, they have little contact with others and, for many, no love and no loving touch. On top of this they are routinely humiliated, despised and insulted, sometimes tortured and considered as animals to be disposed of at will. Whatever horrors some may have committed it is still true that many are innocent; 30% of all people condemned to Death since 1976 have later been released and there is good evidence that many, like Edward Earl Johnson, who are actually executed are innocent. But it doesn't matter to many because they belong to an underclass of those excluded from society and thus from relationship with others. Someone had to pay for the violence of society and what better person to pay than someone who is mentally retarded, black or poor.

Here among the poor you find the finger of God. "The words of the prophets are written on the subway walls and tenement halls,"[174] and whispered in the cellblocks on Death Row.

Visiting Death Row for the first time is unnerving for a middle-class privileged person like me. We were expecting the razor wire, the guard towers, the seemingly endless series of steel gates, the searches, the austerity of the prison, the roll calls, the awful food at the canteen (still much better than that served in the cells); all of these contribute to an intimidating experience which is difficult to anticipate, but we were quite unprepared for the poverty of that corner of northern Florida, poverty not disconnected from Death Row, for it is from the tumble-down shacks and trailers by the roadside, as well as the urban ghettoes, that the inmates come, they belong to an already rejected class, they are non-persons, invisible and faceless. Yet here on Death Row you find qualities lacking in society as a whole; by our third visit, as I was standing in the queue at the canteen window for yet more salty, sugary, fatty fare, a strange thought entered my head. I thought, "I feel at home here." I might well have added, "I wish I was always as much at home in the church."

I ask myself why I felt so at home. Here is part of the answer:

My Friend

> Where does friendship lie?
> The Lord said,
> "Look in all
>   The unlikely places."
> What is love, and why?
> The Lord said,
> "Look at all
>   The unusual faces."
>
> So, looking, by and by
> The Lord said,
> "Here is one of
>   The rejected cases."
> So, hesitant and shy,
> (The Lord said)
> "This is one of
>   My hidden aces."

So, at last, I found a
  Condemned man, killer
  Psychopath, satan-fuelled,
So I found a murderer,
  Mercenary, schizoid,
  Sentence: Death.
And in this (unlikely) man,
  Unusual sure, rejected,
  Trash even, I found
A friend.

So at last I found what
  Is so rare in our
  "Free" world. I found
Loyalty, faithfulness,
  Acceptance, love.
I found a man in the
  Image of God. Creative,
  Generous and kind.
And, having found this
  Man transformed by
  Christ it seems
So harsh to find that
  Cancer chews at
  Every cell, destroys
His body.

And yet I know that
  I at least shall
  Never be the same.
Knowing him I have
  Seen a glimpse of
  God Himself.
And I shall honour him
  In my heart by
  Seeking with yet
More strength to
  Serve the Lord who
  Gave this man to be
My friend.

My sense of being at home certainly wasn't down to the subtlety of
the décor, or the comfort of the furniture or the entertainment on
offer. The answer lies in friendship, and in acceptance. On Death Row

many of those considered non-persons have discovered the essence of personality, which is relationship. You meet first the other visitors. Every weekend and holiday they gather at dawn and wait in a queue. In winter it can be cold, even frosty, in summer it is unbearably hot. In all weathers they wait patiently and accept newcomers readily. We even exchanged addresses with one family who were due to visit Europe; later we discovered that we had given our address to a notorious gangster family. But we were all in the same boat; though not all poor ourselves, we were all at the place of ultimate poverty and powerlessness.

I felt at home because for all the meanness of a few guards, the majority are courteous and respectful and do their best to make the visit a pleasant experience for everyone. They too have struggled to survive in a hostile environment.

I felt at home because of the honesty and reality of many of the relationships on Death Row. Florida is a long way to go to find reality, but it's worth the trip. When I returned from our third visit I wrote an article which I entitled *Charles Globe Ruined my Life.*[175] Charles did nothing of the sort, of course, but the experience of the reality of Death Row has made me intolerant of the pettiness of religion, pettiness with which I was engaging daily. I felt I could no longer get on with religion and eventually resigned my two positions in the church. The same honesty is apparent at LifeLines conferences. When you are faced with execution, your own or that of someone you love, though there is plenty of humour, there's no appetite for triviality. Religion can't help you at this stage, only faith can.

In St Paul's correspondence with the volatile Corinthian church there is a little give-away about genuine relationships, tucked away among praises for the financial generosity of the Macedonian church: "They did not do as we expected, but they gave themselves first to the Lord and then to us in keeping with God's will."[176]

They *gave themselves…* Here's the rub: Honest self-giving is the key to relationships. Paul knew that the giving of money is meaningless unless we have first given ourselves.

TRICIA and Darren are engaged to be married. Tricia and her Mum, Karen, are busy making the arrangements. Everything will be perfect, the silk dress, the venue, the food, the music, the honeymoon, everything must be of the best, it's going to be a great day. Tricia is *excited*. As they make the arrangements, Darren gets to know Karen and there is a spark between them. Then, on the big day, Tricia discovers that her fiancé has been conducting an affair with her mother. Meanwhile Tricia's father, Karen's estranged husband, is making out with Tracey, the chief bridesmaid, and ex-girlfriend of Darren, who is herself engaged to Tricia's brother, Mark. Will Tricia go ahead with the wedding? Wait for the next episode of ....

Soap Operas! When I was the priest in a small Devon village I was approached by an executive of a TV company. She asked if she could spend some time with me as she was researching a new soap opera in a rural setting. There is an urban bias to British politics and I was eager to bang the drum for the countryside so I agreed to show her around the parish, helping her understand how small rural communities tick. How naïve can you get! Then came the confession: This soap was not meant to reflect real life, but was intended as a fantasy. I don't keep up with soap operas, but I don't think this one ever saw the light of day. Many people do, however, live a surrogate life through the characters in Coronation Street or Albert Square. When Susan Carter was imprisoned, in the plot of the radio soap *The Archers,* cars sprouted "Free the Ambridge One" stickers, and questions were asked in parliament; probably they were tongue in cheek, but it was revealing nonetheless.

Perhaps a TV series can be entertaining, but there is always the temptation to live our lives through the lens of the TV camera, thus avoiding real life, rather as the stereotypical Japanese tourist experiences London through a viewfinder. In a TV series we can feel part of a (bogus) community while remaining ourselves totally detached. Unlike a theatre crowd who contribute to the vitality of the performance, a TV audience is not required to give anything of themselves (and anyway the actors have long-since gone home); if they are bored they chat or else get up and make a pot of tea, they can always catch up by reading the tabloids, who report the soaps as much as they report real life.

When I was a musician I disliked recording work, though the extra money came in handy. In the studio there is no audience to take their part in the creation of the music, there is no spark of interaction between player and listener, no self-giving by the audience, and no coughing either for this is a sterile environment. You know too that, when things go wrong, you can always play that bit again, be it a single bar of a whole movement. Since you know you might have to play it all again you hold back some energy for that possibility. Either way recording does not encourage the total self-giving of a really exciting concert where you only get the one chance.

In many so-called relationships in life there is little genuine self-giving. In chapter 7 we met the fictional character Kevin, who seemed to know everyone; but it turned out he hardly knew them at all. Relationships can operate on this level, or worse on the level of who has the right trainers or sweat shirt, or who is part of the "in" group that day. In this there is no commitment, little engagement and a studied avoidance of authenticity; those who admit to depression or financial worries are dropped as fast as the prodigal was dropped by his "friends".[177] Fear of rejection lies behind the lack of honesty.

When I was younger, like many others I used to think that if someone knew the real "me" they wouldn't like or accept me. So I hid the real me and tried to be someone else, with the result that I only got to know people who were not well suited as authentic friends, people who were attracted only to the bogus persona I presented, not the "real me". You can become badly unstuck on this one. You can end up with multiple personae as well, which is embarrassing when, at the same time, you run into Bill, with whom you are an ardent Manchester United supporter, and Fred, with whom you share your enthusiasm for Manchester City. Both may surmise, possibly correctly, that you don't even like football and that they find more common ground between themselves than with you, the pretender.

Some people play their part so convincingly that they themselves are convinced, then they cease to know themselves at all; a TV personality when asked about the difference between his TV persona and the real man replied that there probably wasn't a real person any more. Others are more blatant; overheard in the stalls at The Royal Opera House: "How long have we got to endure tonight?" And the tickets were £160 each! Neither is a good recipe for life let alone relationships.

Relationships begin when I take the risk of knowing myself. What are my deepest desires and longings? What am I really interested in? What am I passionate about? What do I loathe? I learn to own these likes and loves and longings, even when I think they may not be acceptable; I learn to love myself with all my foibles. In order to do this well I have to abandon pretence, stop spending my money on things I can't afford and don't need to impress people I don't like. If I really like train spotting I will go for it.

The next step is the risky, and perhaps gradual, revelation of this real but intensely vulnerable person to someone else. "They did not do as we expected, but they gave themselves first to the Lord and then to us in keeping with God's will."

Self-giving is risky. A scene in *Tess of the d'Urbervilles* illustrates. Angel Clare and Tess are newly-married. Angel confesses to Tess that he had previously "plunged into eight-and-forty hours' dissipation with a stranger,"[178] and asks for Tess' forgiveness, which she freely gives. Emboldened by Angel's confession Tess herself confesses to her own disastrous liason with Alec d'Urberville and asks for Angel's forgiveness. Such is not forthcoming, however, and there and then the marriage ends. Self-giving is risky. Every time we reveal something of ourselves to another we take the risk of rejection. But just as adventures of necessity involve risk (chapter 5), so relationships, also of necessity, involve risk. The risk-free relationship is a sterile as the risk-free adventure.

I wonder how much of this genuine (and risky) self-giving goes on in church congregations today? If you're unsure about yours you could try these questions:

- You are about to go bankrupt. Where and from whom do you seek help?
- You are employed as a diver on an oil-rig. You also have a passion for ballet. With whom do you share your passion?
- Though otherwise healthy you have acquired an embarrassing disease. Your church offers a healing service. Do you go forward and ask for healing?
- You live an honest and chaste life but you are attracted sexually to people of the same gender. Can you share this, and with whom?
- You have a tendency to depression. Who knows about it?

Most people hide these perhaps uncomfortable truths about themselves, especially from members of their church, feigning respectability in their place. "How are you?" they ask. "I'm, fine," I reply. It becomes automatic; indeed I once went to the doctor, who asked, "How are you?" "I'm fine," I said, to which the doctor replied, quick as a flash, "Then why are you here?"

Why do we hide these important parts of ourselves? Could it be because we do not trust our sisters and brothers in Christ, thus we cannot "give ourselves" to the fellowship? How far is that from the, perhaps idealised, picture of the Apostolic Church in the New Testament?

> "All the believers were together and had everything in common."[179]

> "All the believers were one in heart and mind."[180]

> "They did not do as we expected, but they gave themselves first to the Lord and then to us in keeping with God's will."[181]

Do not imagine, when Luke writes, "the believers were one in heart and mind" that he intends us to believe they were all alike. When Jesus chose twelve friends to accompany Him, He chose a bunch of fishermen. To these original four He added, incongruously, a terrorist, "Simon who was called the Zealot,"[182] and alongside him, Levi (or Matthew) the collaborator.[183] Then there was Thomas, the doubter, though I think this an unfair designation[184] and alongside him Judas, the traitor.[185] And, of course, there were the forgotten women, Mary Magdalene with her questionable past, along with the well-to-do women who supported Jesus.[186] What a rag-tag of a bunch. Before very long the church had grown to include the hated Gentiles as well!

There are several marks of an authentic Christian fellowship, but one stands out: A genuine fellowship makes room for all types: university professors jostle with the mentally handicapped, conservatives befriend socialists, sportsmen mingle with paraplegics, young and old, black and white, men and women all rub along and – yes – evangelicals, catholics, charismatics and liberals co-exist happily.

IN chapter 7 we explored the mystery of human relationships; we discovered that the more you get to know another the less you seem to know them. This is not an invitation to stop trying or to remain at a superficial level in our relationships, in genuine relationships we plunge together into the mystery of those, including ourselves, made in the image of God.[187]

I often discuss my faith with those who are sceptical, agnostics or atheists among them. The conversation often takes in the contradictions in the Bible, the absurdity of some Christian doctrines, the abuses apparent in church history, the hypocrisy of church members, and much more. I usually try to halt these fruitless discussions by saying something like this, "Faith is not about doctrines, it's about relationship." In human relationships we put up with, and even welcome, all sorts of contradictions, paradoxes, absurdities and unattractive traits. We can be friends with people quite unlike ourselves, a good example is the friendship between the Mayor and Monsignor Quixote in a lovely and hilarious novel by Graham Greene[188] which, though fiction, was inspired by a living Spanish priest. In fact difference, absurdities and paradoxes make relationships even more interesting; who wants a friend like a character in a soap opera, who always reacts in the same way, is always consistent, and consistently dull? Who wants a friend who always agrees with you and echoes your every word and thought? Inflexible creeds, doctrines, canon law can teach us religion, relationships teach us faith.

———————•◦•———————

READERS of a nervous disposition will want to skip this section because in it I am going to discuss one of the great taboos of 21ˢᵗ Century life. I don't mean sex; nowadays it's perfectly acceptable to discuss the finer points of love-making quite openly. Neither am I talking about money; unless we are bankrupt, we are usually quite open about our salaries and investments. Neither am I talking about death which is an unpleasant subject and usually avoided. I mean commitment.

Commitment is not in vogue. Imagine a child, we'll call her Charlotte, anticipating her seventh birthday. Charlotte is *excited*. Her mother has booked the village hall, sent out the invitations, engaged the enter-tainer, baked for a week, blown up countless balloons and bought expensive party bags. The day which seemed an eternity away finally arrives. Charlotte's mother spends the morning making final prepara-tions; the clock creeps round the dial until at last it strikes four. The music starts to play, the juggler is poised with his balls and the kettle whistles merrily. There is one ingredient missing, guests. No one arrives. Six hours later, or so it seems, at 4.30, Charlotte's mother is getting nervous. She telephones Charlotte's great friend, Emily. "Sorry," says her mother, "Emily's gone to see her aunt today." Lizzie's mother tells a similar story; Amelia has gone to the theatre with her father, while Annabel has popped over to Orlando for half-term. At last the ghastly truth dawns, no one is coming to Charlotte's party, all the guests have accepted a better offer. You will recognise the story, of course, because Jesus told it 2000 years ago.[189] *Plus ça change.* In His story only the excuses differ, one guest had bought a field, another had bought five yoke of oxen, and yet another had just got married. It seems that lack of commitment is not a new phenomenon.

When I was about five years old I was invited to the joint birthday party of twin classmates; I was thrilled to be invited because the twins were regarded as tough in our school and an invitation to their party would do my social standing no harm at all. But that weekend the funfair came to town, and it so happened that the only time someone could take me was at exactly the time of the twins' party. How I grumbled, moaned, cried to be allowed to go to the fair. All to no avail. "You accepted the invitation," my mother said, "and you must go." How wise she was. It was a great party too.

Sadly Charlotte's experience is all too common as each day people accept the best available offer rather than that to which they were committed. But real friendship requires unconditional commitment. That means dependability, that means stickability, that means unconditional faithfulness whatever may happen. Without these qualities there is no friendship.

Imagine the opposite. Beverly's son was accused and charged with capital murder. He was never brought to trial, the actual killer confessed six days before. However Beverly "was asked to leave her church... Beverly's church contacted her after charges were dismissed against her son, but she has not returned to church."[190] I wonder why not?

The boot is often on the other foot too, as the lame excuses for individuals not being in church show. Either way we are looking at conditional friendship and there is no such thing. Friendship is unconditional, non-judgemental and it perseveres.

I MENTIONED above that sex is no longer a taboo in western society. Before we close this chapter on relationships we may well reflect on this particularly intimate expression of love, for, like it or not, human beings are sexual creatures. Over the years, since Augustine projected his sexual hang-ups on the western church in the 4th Century, sex has been thought of as sinful, tolerated in marriage for the purpose of procreation, but otherwise to be avoided. In fact, sin and sex are sometimes thought to be synonyms. As in the old song:

> I long to sin
> With Eleanor Glynn
> On a tiger-skin.

In an attempt to redress the balance Morton and Barbara Kelsey call sex sacramental, in other words holy.[191] We have already seen in chapter 2 that John of the Cross, though celibate, conceived of faith in terms of erotic love. The Song of Songs, John's favourite Scriptural text, while interpreted as allegory by an embarrassed Christian church, is at its most immediate an erotic poem of startling sensuality and candour.

The problem today is that sexual intercourse is too often divorced from *eros* and the sexual act wrenched away from friendship, love and commitment. Casual sex can be fun at the time, but it leaves you feeling empty; it dehumanises and, as the rewards decline, can become addictive. When physical union is disconnected from the quest for spiritual union it becomes merely a thrill with diminishing returns. Philip Yancey comments:

> When a society so completely blocks the human thirst for transcendence, should we be surprised that such longings reroute themselves into an expression of mere physicality? Maybe the problem is not that people are getting naked, but that they aren't getting naked enough: we stop at the skin instead of going deeper, into the soul.[192]

The integrity of the personality demands that physical union is an expression of actual intimacy, an act in which two human beings are immersed in each other until they grow into complete union with each other. As such, sexual intercourse is a sign, a sacrament of the soul's union with God.

Endnotes

[170] See, among others: *Death of Innocents* Sister Helen Prejean (Canterbury Press 2006), *The Innocent Man* John Grisham (Century 2006) and *The Biblical Truth About America's Death Penalty* Dale S Recinella (Northeastern University Press 2004)
[171] www.iwasinprison.org
[172] See for example 1 Corinthians 12:13
[173] Luke 6:20

[174] *The Sound of Silence* Paul Simon and Art Garfunkel

[175] This illustrated article appeared in the *Church Times* on 20th April 2007 under the tabloid-style headline "Florida wants to kill my pen pal."

[176] 2 Corinthians 8:5

[177] Luke 15:16

[178] *Tess of the d'Urbervilles* Thomas Hardy (Oxford 1998 edition p 221)

[179] Acts 2:44 This does not apply only to material possessions.

[180] Acts 4:32

[181] 2 Corinthians 8:5

[182] Luke 6:15

[183] Luke 5:27f

[184] John 20:24-27 Contrast John 11:16

[185] Luke 6:16

[186] Luke 8:1-3

[187] Genesis 1:27

[188] *Monsignor Quixote* Graham Greene (Vintage Classics 2006)

[189] Matthew 22:1-14, Luke 14:15-21

[190] *Hidden Victims* Susan F Sharp (Rutgers University Press 2005 pp 122f)

[191] *Sacrament of Sexuality* Morton and Barbara Kelsey (Element 1986)

[192] *Finding God in Unexpected Places* Philip Yancey (Hodder and Stoughton 2002 p 16)

Chapter 10
FAITH IN JESUS

The LORD would speak to Moses face to face, as a man speaks with his friend.[193]

I no longer call you servants, because a servant does not know his master's business. Instead, I have called you friends.[194]

Dear friends, now we are children of God.[195]

> Jesus, my Shepherd, Brother, Friend,
> My Prophet, Priest and King,
> My Lord, my Life, my Way, my End,
> Accept the praise I bring.[196]

I'M sitting down to write a letter. In these days of text messages and emails that's an unusual activity, but rewarding nonetheless. What's more, this is not a letter to my bank, nor is it a job application, nor a circular letter to tuck in my Christmas cards. This is a hand-written personal letter. Before the age of the telephone and internet this was the way people at a distance communicated with each other.

Letter writing is fast becoming a lost skill. Once it was a great art form, the letters of the great and good are a wonderful resource for the biographer, people will write words in a personal letter which they wouldn't dream of writing in a book or newspaper article. When we look at the letters of famous people we can see a side of them which was previously hidden. Thank God, for example, for the little private letter from Paul to Philemon, preserved for us in the New Testament.

So, I'm sitting down to write a letter. I am not too concerned with structure, grammar, spelling or even handwriting, this is not a job application after all. I am writing down some of the events of the day and what I noticed and how I felt; I am revealing a little about myself, my history, my family, my hopes, my fears, my dreams, my plans, my likes, dislikes, loves and loathings, I am mentioning my concerns for others, and above all I am appreciating the person to whom I am writing.

To whom is this letter addressed? It could be a love letter to my wife; we already have a bundle of love letters which we wrote to each other during a time of separation in our courtship, and very precious they are too, they are the record of a slowly growing love; we add to them when we go on retreat. It could be a letter to a precious friend, trying to say something profound about our friendship, better said in a letter than on the telephone. It could be a letter to my best friend in all the universe.

And what happens when we receive such a letter? Eagerly we have waited for the sound of the postman, the clunk of the letter box, the dull thud of letters on the mat. Urgently we have rushed to the front door and hastily placed on one side the bank statements, bills and junk mail, looking for the hand-writing we know so well. We have torn open the letter and devoured the contents, we have touched it, we have smelt it, we have laughed, we have cried, we have shouted for joy. Then we have placed it on one side, made a cup of coffee and sat down to really digest the precious words. Later in the day we read it again and then we sit down to write a reply. Perhaps, if we are really sentimental, we may sleep with the letter under the pillow, or by the bed.

It's easy to send a text or email. Writing a letter requires effort, time, commitment; it is not instant but it is an expression of friendship and love.

———•◦•———

OVER the last nine chapters we have considered a number of metaphors for faith used as a way of attempting the impossible, a description of the indescribable, that is the relationship of the soul to God. We have considered story, music, dance, adventure, play, mystery, discipline and relationship; there could have been more, for example dreams, drama or mime. Now at last we arrive at the kernel of it all; relationship with Jesus though we have used relationship in chapter 9 as metaphor, is the actual and irreducible nucleus of faith. Faith is the journey of the soul towards union with God in Jesus Christ. It is a long journey, it is not accomplished in an afternoon. True friendship does not blossom in a night; like a rose, once it is grafted onto the stock it takes time, tender care and patience, to grow and flower. Friends do not release genuine friendship instantly.

———————•◦•———————

ALL those who are "in Christ" have a story to tell, a story of a patiently growing friendship with Jesus. You have read quite a bit of mine already. For some their story will include a great moment of revelation similar to Saul of Tarsus' experience on the Damascus Road,[197] while others will have experienced a much more gradual awakening. Some may have started out in a blaze of enthusiasm, then drifted away only to return to the patient effort of faith later on. Whatever our own experience we should remember that friendship, like good wine, takes years to mature; even Saul's conversion was not the work of an instant.

We first meet Saul in Acts 7:58 where he is the driving force behind the stoning to death of Stephen, the first martyr. We read: "Saul was there, giving approval to his death."[198] The author of Acts has already remarked that, at Stephen's trial "they saw that his face was like the face of an angel."[199] I suggest that he got that from an eye-witness, probably Paul (Saul) himself; it is likely that the serene face of Stephen under intense persecution burned into Saul's brain; how could Stephen the heretic know the peace Saul the orthodox Pharisee craved? In a vain attempt to erase the image of Stephen's saintly death Saul was driven to ever greater lengths, trying to stamp out the fledgling Christian faith. At last, after a considerable time, he experienced some sort of breakdown. But even then Saul the Pharisee was not instantly transformed into Paul the Apostle. That transformation from enemy to friend of

Jesus took many years.[200] Friendship is like that, it takes time to grow, and it takes commitment and effort too. We focus on Paul because we shall return to him at the end of the chapter.

I HAVE mentioned the letter writing between Monica, my wife, and I. Our friendship with Charles is, of necessity also carried on mainly through letters, twice a week or so another drops on the mat containing perhaps a card, or a cartoon, or pictures, poems and, of course, beautiful letters. Death Row prisoners in Florida have no access to the internet or mobile phones.

There is, too, another correspondence we may engage in: One of the most precious tools available for our walk of faith is the love correspondence with God we call a spiritual journal. We may imagine, if we can imagine Him as a divine Lover, that He receives this correspondence with unbridled enthusiasm. I have kept a journal for decades. It is a record of a deepening friendship, a love affair even, with Jesus. What a remarkable phrase that is, read it again: a love affair with Jesus. One simple device for keeping a journal is to write a love letter to God. Since a journal is entirely private these letters can be as candid as you like and as corny, lovers understand such things. They can also meander aimlessly, using poor grammar, spelling and punctuation, and the handwriting doesn't much matter either. You can even write what you imagine may be God's reply, strange how God's handwriting is so similar to my own! As I re-read my journal I find a candid record of a relationship with a person, with all our ups and downs, joys and sorrows. I treasure this correspondence as I treasure letters from Monica or from Charles. I will no more quote from it than I would quote from my love letters to my wife, for God is indeed my lover too, and my intimate friend. How dare we call Jesus an intimate friend? Yet that is what, through grace, He is. John of the Cross, as we saw in chapter 2, perceived his relationship with God as a passionate love affair in which the divine Lover and His beloved pursue one another until, after many a dark night of separation, they finally enter into eternal union. This is strong stuff and impossible to understand fully. There are a number of stumbling blocks for us in the western world before we dare approach God as a Lover.

------◆------

WHEN my father was trying to teach me how to practice the piano, a skill I never mastered, he used to say that every time you made a mistake it was essential to unlearn that mistake immediately before it becomes a habit; you can only learn the right way when you have unlearnt the wrong way. That applies to everything in life. When I started the bassoon I began on an old French instrument, an instrument already obsolete outside France. Later, when I moved onto a contemporary German instrument, I had to unlearn many of those techniques which had already become a habit. Years later I could still slip into the old French fingerings. For many of us in the west, before we can learn that God in Jesus is our divine Lover, we have to unlearn much ingrained suspicion and fear.

In the west, at least, and among people in my generation, we had grown accustomed to thinking of God as a sort of celestial schoolmaster in gown and mortar board; some will imagine a Jimmy Edwards type with his handlebar moustaches but without the concealed good nature, peering over the balcony of heaven, cane in hand, simply longing for an excuse to utilise the instrument of chastisement. At my prep. school, in Devon, the headmaster was very free with the cane, even for the "crime" of leaving bathing trunks on the washing line. I suppose we saw him as a type of God and projected the image onto the real thing. Getting caned for a minor "offence" was quickly forgotten, but we also knew that for really serious offences we could be expelled, excluded, and never allowed back; we may even have to go to an Approved School, like the one down the road, or so we imagined. We visited that Approved School each year, to make use of their boxing ring. It was a grim place, reminiscent of Dotheboys Hall, its stark walls and harsh discipline were to be avoided at all costs.

So we have grown accustomed to comparing God to the headmaster, imagining that Christianity is about retrieving your bathing trunks before supper, being "good", keeping your nose clean and doing the best we can or else risking a good beating or, should we stray too far, permanent exclusion in the hell of an everlasting Approved School. It is, we think, about doing enough and not getting caught, about being respectable and not allowing our vulnerability to show, so that by all means we avoid a terrible fate.

This goes deep. Some years ago I preached a passionate sermon about the free grace of God, grace which does not count our sins against us, grace which demands only love in return and which draws us into a love relationship with God in Jesus. Salvation, I thundered, is not about effort and good works, achievement or good marks, but about the unmerited but freely-given love of God for each of us. It is always chastening when you fail to communicate, but on this occasion one response really took the biscuit; an elderly lady shook my hand after the service and said, "lovely sermon, Vicar. It's like I say, you can only do your best." Grrrrrr!

I realised at an early age that doing my best was not going to be good enough. Again at prep. school there were three large boards in the hall. Everyone's name appeared on one of these boards and alongside each name pins were stuck, red pins were good marks, blue were bad, and it was imperative to acquire more reds than blues or there would be trouble. But try as I might, the blues always seemed to creep ahead. So, as an adolescent, I quickly concluded that, since I was quite incapable of achieving the impossible standards God required I may as well stop trying and enjoy this life while I may before being condemned to the torments of hell. God, it seemed, was watching my every move like Orwell's "Big Brother"; and, like Big Brother, He seemed perfectly happy in His good time to dispatch me to Room 101 where I would meet the ultimate horror, (curious how both Big Brother and Room 101 have become quite inappropriate titles of TV programmes). Even if we don't hold quite such a graphic view of a stern God, we may consider that God is at best unconcerned with our life.

Many cannot see God as anything other than a grotesque monster. They look at the abuses of the Christian Church over the years, the religious wars and persecutions, the manipulation of the vulnerable; they look at the cases of child abuse in religious institutions which is only now coming to light; they look at some of the more frightening passages in the Old Testament and cannot accept that God could be a God of Love. Those who can see only the abuses have a great deal to unlearn before they can understand the God of Love. Those ingrained images take a lot of unlearning, but here's an attempt:

Charity

There is a lie, that God (if God there be)
Is distant, unconcerned with human misery;
His dispassionate eyes watch uncaringly as we,
With atom bomb and poison gas, desecrate human life.
Perhaps he has a flutter with a neighbouring god
On the outcome of these tragic wars. Or does the ghastly sod
Just smash what he has made like spoiled child?

And, since there be no charity from above,
Human beings have learnt to grab and push and shove.
No time to take delight in simple natural things.
A moment's peace, and ruthless rival steals ahead
And market leader, overnight, takeover dreads.
The air is thick with sounds of rats and rolling heads
And hospitals are overfull with victims of the hideous race.

Yet those who make a space, women and men of bravery
The ones with eyes to see, perceive a sermon in a tree.
Saints and sinners both alike may ponder on their history
And, with surprised delight, find the hand of God
In unexpected crannies of the past. They find
Subtle vision, fleeting glimpse (though they once were blind)
And moments of grace perceived with hindsight's eye.

And since God cares and there is ample charity
We may be free to live and love for all eternity,
And stock exchange may rise and fall and I care not a whit.
Life may deal some crushing blows: Tempest, earthquake, flood,
Inhumanity, violent deeds, petty meannesses and crime,
Altercation, family strife, hatred happen all the time.
Still I am God's and He is mine and charity rules the world.

At the crucial points in life I have, "with surprised delight, [found] the hand of God… moments of grace…" I have had to struggle to unlearn the notion of a harsh and judgemental God to make space to learn that God is a God of love (charity in the archaic language of my poem) and that He draws me into His friendship.

In his letter to the Ephesians Paul offers a prayer that his readers may similarly know the love of God; he prays:

> that Christ may dwell in your hearts through faith. And I pray that you, being rooted and established in love, may have power, together with all the saints, to grasp how wide and long and high and deep is the love of Christ, and to know this love, which surpasses knowledge – that you may be filled to the measure of all the fullness of God.[201]

This is not easy. Those of us who don't see God as a tyrant nevertheless feel utterly unworthy of friendship with so mighty a person as God.

"Who am I?" we may say to ourselves. The sense of unworthiness is captured by George Herbert in his poem entitled, simply, *Love*, a dialogue between the soul and Love.

> Love bade me welcome: yet my soul drew back,
>> Guilty of dust and sin.
> But quick-ey'd Love, observing me grow slack
>> From my first entrance in,
> Drew nearer to me, sweetly questioning,
>> If I lack'd anything.
>
> A guest, I answer'd, worthy to be here:
>> Love said, You shall be he.
> I the unkind, ungrateful? Ah my dear,
>> I cannot look on thee.
> Love took my hand, and smiling did reply,
>> Who made the eyes but I?

Truth Lord, but I have marr'd them: let my shame
    Go where it doth deserve.
And know you not, says Love, who bore the blame?
    My dear, then I will serve.
You must sit down, says Love, and taste my meat:
    So I did sit and eat.

As friends of Jesus our vocation is a far higher calling than merely to serve, we are called to sit at high table with the one who calls us "Friend".

Much less subtle, but making the same point, is a dialect poem by Geoffrey Studdert Kennedy (Woodbine Willie) entitled *Well?* The verse speaks of the hell-fire preaching of a Great War chaplain, which leads a simple soldier to ponder his failings. He imagines himself at the judgement seat:

And then at last 'E said one word,
    'E just said one word – "Well?"
And I said in a funny voice,
    "Please can I go to 'Ell?"
And 'E stood there and looked at me,
    And 'E kind o' seemed to grow,
Till 'E shone like the sun above my 'ead,
    And then 'E answered "No,
You can't ..."[202]

The Christian faith is relationship with Christ. In our friendship with Him we discover that God is not some tyrant in the sky, but a warm and loving friend whose friendship surpasses any earthly friendship and whose love transcends human love. No wonder Paul can write to the Philippians, "I want to know Christ..."[203] So do I, because the little I know makes me want to grow into deeper knowledge, fellowship, friendship and ultimately into union with Him.

***

KNOWING God in a personal relationship has always been God's plan for all people. The history of God's people can be viewed as the history of a covenant between God and His people. This covenant was established with Abraham,[204] the father of faith, and constantly renewed throughout the Old Testament. Gradually the Jews, or at least their prophets, recognised that this covenant was not exclusively a covenant with the Jews themselves, but rather they were to be the channel for God's covenant love of all people.[205] Sadly the terms of the Old Covenant, mild as they were, were too much for fragile humans and our failure to keep to them led to a breach between humanity and God. So God, the divine Lover who never gives up, established a new covenant, in which He not only fulfilled His side of the deal, but bore the burden of our failure to keep our side of it, and thus re-established the broken relationship. It is as if He stole into that school hall at dead of night and removed all the blue pins, leaving only the red, but in consequence He had to suffer the exclusion that the weight of those blue pins demanded, for He "bore the blame" for them all.

Long before Jesus' birth the prophet Jeremiah foresaw God's act of love and wrote the passage which predicts the New Covenant:

> "The time is coming," declares the LORD, "when I will make a new covenant with the house of Israel and with the house of Judah... This is the covenant ... I will be their God and they will be my people. No longer will a man teach his neighbour, or a man his brother, saying, 'Know the LORD,' because they will all know me, from the least of them to the greatest..."[206]

The author of Hebrews regarded this passage as so important he quoted it in full,[207] drawing the conclusion that Jesus has ushered in this promised new covenant. Since there is a new covenant the old is rendered obsolete. The old covenant which had proved impossible for humans to keep was consigned to the dustbin in a supreme act of grace; the relationship is restored, a relationship of unbreakable love and friendship between us and God Himself, made possible by the sacrifice of Jesus Christ on the Cross.

SO we come almost to the end of this brief book. What more can we say, other than God is Love, and His love is expressed in a love relationship with us which will never come to an end? He is the most trustworthy friend you'll ever know and His name is Love.

> Love is patient, love is kind. It does not envy, it does not boast... it is not easily angered, it keeps no record of wrongs... It always protects, always trusts, always hopes, always perseveres. Love never fails.[208]

This could be a little thumbnail sketch of Jesus, whose name is Love. Try it:

> Jesus is patient, Jesus is kind. He does not envy, He does not boast... He is not easily angered, He keeps no record of wrongs... He always protects, always trusts, always hopes, always perseveres. Jesus never fails.

Then, looking forward to complete union with the object of his love Paul writes:

> Now we see but a poor reflection as in a mirror; then we shall see face to face. Now I know in part; then I shall know fully, even as I am fully known.[209]

FULLY known, warts and all, and yet fully loved, just as we are. This is the heart of the Christian faith.

Endnotes

[193] Exodus 33:11
[194] John 15:15
[195] 1 John 3:2
[196] *How Sweet the Name of Jesus Sounds* John Newton (in most hymnals)

[197] Acts 9:1-19; 22:3-16; 26:12-18

[198] Acts 8:1

[199] Acts 6:15

[200] Galatians 1:13-24

[201] Ephesians 3:16-19

[202] *Well?* G Studdert Kennedy in *The Unutterable Beauty* (Mowbray 1983 p 124)

[203] Philippians 3:10

[204] Genesis 15

[205] See e.g. Jonah and Isaiah 42:6, 49:6

[206] Jeremiah 31:31-34

[207] Hebrews 8:8-12

[208] 1 Corinthians 13:4-8

Chapter 11
CONCLUSION

CHAPTER 1 set out the aims of this book. We began with the story of the Obsession and wondered what the significance of the little hawthorn might be. Then we looked at a fragment of a poem entitled *The House* and wondered about the identity of the strange visitor. Next the thought was the silences in music and we wondered what might be in the gaps of faith. We asked the question, "What is the antidote to religion?" We also saw faith as a journey and together we have been on a journey through a variety of metaphors.

AT the end of this stage of our journey we can ask again, "What is the antidote to religion?" The title of this book gives the game away, faith is the antidote, faith enables us to put aside religious wars and bad feeling, to put away death and live, to laugh, love and suck the juice out of life. But I have tried to show, too, that the counter to religion is in a completely different way of perceiving. Truth is not enshrined in doctrines, creeds or formulae, it is found in the elusive arts of story, poetry, music, dance. Truth is found in dreams and only when you push the boat out without guarantees to discover in the risk of adventure, and on the journey to who knows where, that life makes sense. Science has its uses, but it cannot answer all our questions, God is found not in science, nor in philosophy, but in mystery. The answers to life are found on the blank pages at the end of this book, in the gaps, where no one has thought to look. When the widow swept her house in search of her lost coin[210] she had to look in all the least likely places. She had already looked behind the sofa, in the little mug full of odds and ends on the drainer and in the pockets of her housecoat. In the end she found the elusive coin in the gaps between the floorboards. In the gaps, that is where we find faith.

God's sense of humour prompts Him to hide treasure in improbable places, just like the children's party game. When God appointed David King of Israel in place of Saul He told Samuel to reject the older brothers. In the end God appointed the youngest, the least likely.[211] God has been doing the same ever since. Jesus chose uncouth fishermen to be His closest friends, and a host of unlikely characters to accompany them. He selected Saul of Tarsus to take the Gospel message to the Gentiles, themselves unlikely candidates. In the end God even chose you who are reading this book, unlikely as that may seem, to be His disciple; and he chose me too, even less likely!

To perceive God we need eyes to see and ears to hear, we need a sixth sense, an intuitive and questing soul and the courage to explore the gaps, the deep recesses of the soul where no one ever goes. We need the breadth of mind to be able to hold on to paradox without needing to resolve it, we need the humility to know that we are finite beings grappling with an infinite God.

When we fail to perceive we are like those addressed by the prophet Isaiah:

> Be ever hearing, but never understanding; be ever seeing, but never perceiving. Make the heart of the people calloused; make their ears dull and close their eyes. Otherwise they might see with their eyes, hear with their ears, understand with their hearts, and turn and be healed.[212]

There are those today who listen but don't hear, who look but don't see, who ask but don't understand; these are as likely to be religious people as bigoted scientists, either way they are looking in the likely places and ignoring those hidden nooks and crannies where God loves to hide His treasure. But those who are willing to open their eyes and ears, to open hearts as well as minds may claim the promise of Jesus:

Ask, and it will be given to you; seek and you will find; knock and the door will be opened to you.[213]

THEN there was the strange visitor in the fragment of the poem, *The House*. Who is the man, and what was he doing, saying, being during his time in "the house"? Here is the full version.

The House

In some street there's a house,
     Somewhere.
Just an ordinary house, small
     Rather dark.
But inside there are rooms beyond
Curtained rooms
Where no one ever goes.

One night a man arrives and stays awhile.
The fire burns brighter for his presence.
Four long weeks he labours, transforming
All he sees, piece by piece.
The small garden blooms and blossoms and
Before my eyes grows into a vast wonderland
With precious stones for gravel paths and
River flowing by. Cherry, willow, beech
Grow there, and cedar offers welcome shade.

Within: a spacious parlour's filled with light.
Broad stairway leads to wondrous memory rooms
And attics full of happy childhood things.
Those curtained rooms, now evil-purged, are sealed.
As you'd expect there is a view
But not a street in sight, instead
The merest glimpse of heaven.

In the house guests are welcome but
Two treasured guests, a mother and her
Son, may come and go at will.
Their presence makes the house a home
And more, a gateway to the eternal dance
In heaven.

The poem speaks of transformation. It is in fact a record of the *Spiritual Exercises of Ignatius Loyola* which I made in a thirty-day retreat in 2001. What the visitor did and said to me during those thirty days is deeply personal; but this same visitor can visit your "house" and transform it too, He can turn the dullness of your life into brilliance, He can open your eyes to see His wonders in the everyday.

WE end where we began, with the little hawthorn. Religious people are often really "nice" people. People of faith, however, often have a little bit of prickle to them as well. Without that little bit of prickle to pop the bubble of their own pomposity, earnestness, seriousness they will succumb to terminal dullness or terrifying fanaticism.

In the end the thorns are not intended to puncture the confidence of others, but to tackle the obsessions of our own religiosity, and so to clear the way for the joyful, life-giving, laughter-filled, darkness-defying, death-denying, zest-filled life of eternity, lived in company with the best friend you'll ever have, the goal of faith, Jesus Christ, the Son of God.

Endnotes

[209] 1 Corinthians 13:12
[210] Luke 15:8-10
[211] 1 Samuel 16:1-13
[212] Isaiah 6:9f
[213] Matthew 7:7

Printed in the United Kingdom by
Lightning Source UK Ltd., Milton Keynes
137697UK00001B/31-90/P